# OZARK LAD
# TO THE
# SOUTH PACIFIC

## Following a young boy from the Ozarks
## Into World War II

### By Glen Morton Harpham

# Ozark Lad to the South Pacific
Following a young boy from the Ozarks
Into World War II
Glen Harpham

© 2020 Emmanuel Books, LLC.
All rights reserved. No part of this publication may be reproduced, stored in a retrieval system or transmitted in any form or by any means, electronic, mechanical, photocopying, recording or otherwise without the prior permission of the publisher or in accordance with the provisions of the Copyright, Designs and Patents Act 1988 or under the terms of any license permitting limited copying issued by the Copyright Licensing Agency.

**Published by:**
Emmanuel Books, LLC
34509 Globe School Ave.
Edwards, MO, USA

**Typesetting:** Times New Roman
**Cover Design:** Robert Adams

A CIP record for this book is available from the Library of Congress Cataloging-in-Publication Data

ISBN-978-1-7331211-0-1 (HC)
ISBN-978-1-7331211-5-6 (PB)

Printed in the United States of America

**Copyright 2020**
**Glen Harpham**

# Prologue

The Harpham family lived in England in the early 1800s. They were a well-established family in England. There was a village bearing their name. Charles Harpham was born July 10, 1814 in England. His wife Ann was born May 15, 1818. Four of their children were born in England. Jane was born in 1838, John was born in 1840, Annie was born in 1842, and Susanna came along in 1844.

In the late forties or early fifties Charles loaded up on a big ship and headed to the good old U.S.A. Susanna shared some stories with her children and grandchildren about her family and the trip over. She recorded that her mother Ann Harpham was the niece of the British Royal Duke of Gloucester. A duke was similar to a governor in our country. This British family had great estate including a number of horses and a large amount of property.

Susanna had a terrifying experience coming to the new country. She reported that she became very ill on the trip. She became so ill that the captain was going to throw her overboard. The ship was surrounded by large fish, just waiting to eat anything good that might be thrown overboard. Her mother pleaded for her life and with the help of one of the crewmen, they convinced the captain not to throw her overboard. So they all arrived safely on the other side.

They first settled in Dane County, Wisconsin. They lived there for only a short while. Their last child, Charles Wesley, was born in 1854 in Watertown, Wisconsin.

They soon moved to Sullivan County, Missouri. During the early 1860s the Civil War was just getting started. President Lincoln asked for volunteers for the union army. At the age of 46 years Charles volunteered. He joined in August of 1861. He only got to serve a few months. He was wounded while in the army and was disabled. He was mustered out November 6, 1862 at Spring River, Missouri. His health was bad for several years after he got out of the army.

When the 1880 census was taken, Charles Wesley, the youngest son of Charles Harpham, was farming in Sullivan County, Missouri. Also his wife Charlotte (Long) Harpham and their daughter Daisy D. lived there. They had five children from about 1878 to 1892.

Charles Wesley decided it was time to make a move. So they loaded everything they owned on two boxcars and headed south to Lowry City, Missouri. There they unloaded and put all their belongings on wagons pulled by teams. They tied the old milk cow on the back of the wagon to lead. Then the older kids rounded up all the other livestock, cows mostly, and headed east when they left Lowry City. They came to a place in the river called Brown Ford. There were no bridges at that time. It had been raining quite a bit, so the river was up. They had to camp out for a day or two before they could get across the river.

Finally the river went down and they could get across. They got the livestock, wagon, kids and everything else across the river. They were on their way once again. It was sure slow going. The wagon was loaded heavy and the cows were getting tired and didn't have much to eat. They were lucky to make five or six miles a day. They would stop and rest the team, cows, and themselves. It would take quite a while for the livestock to eat. All they had was grass or weeds. The family didn't have much to eat either. They could try to get a fish or some wild game depending on where they were at the time.

They made lots of stops between Lowry City and Edwards, Missouri. Charles Wesley tried to buy some land along the way, but it was always more money than he had. By this time several weeks had gone by. The team, livestock, and everyone was tired and worn out. There had been some sickness along the way.

They finally made it to Benton County. They stopped at Turkey Creek for the night and there, Charles Wesley met Mr. W.E.S. He owned a lot of land up and down Turkey Creek and it was for sale, but he wanted eight hundred dollars for the farm Charles Wesley wanted. He didn't have quite enough money to buy it.

So after they rested up a little they moved on toward Edwards, Missouri. They got to Deer Creek. They stopped again and set up camp to rest. Charles Wesley and the boys would get out and tried to find some wild game to eat. Sometimes they could and some places there wasn't much to hunt.

After a couple of days rest they moved on south of Edwards. When they had gone about five miles they came to a place where Charles Wesley could homestead. There was forty acres he could buy from the government and there was other land that he could buy that bordered it on all sides. This became the home of the Harpham family and at this time it still is in the Harpham family.

One hundred and some years ago when Charles Wesley settled at Edwards the whole family had to make a lot of changes and a lot of sacrifices. Times were really hard back in those days. About all you had to live on was what you got off the family farm. You had to grow all of your vegetables. You had to raise all your meat, except for the wild game. People had to live kind of like the birds do. They just depended on God to supply their food and needs.

Well, anyway, it was a struggle to survive those bad years. Charles Wesley was my grandpa. I talked to him quite a bit about the old days. He had lots of stories to tell about how bad it really was. The average family today couldn't have made it through all the hardships they went through.

Grandpa said that as bad as it was, it was the greatest thing he had ever done and if it were to do over he would do it again. He always said it was great to be able to help and be a part of developing this area of Missouri. He helped get better roads in and around Edwards. He was a road commissioner for several years. He helped get several county schools in different places. He helped in getting small country stores located. Most every county had a little country store within seven or eight miles of each other.

People went to town in a team and wagon. They didn't buy much. There wasn't much to buy, just get their corn ground so they could make bread. You didn't need much more, maybe a little coffee, sugar and a little kerosene for the lamps.

By this time the Harpham family was getting pretty established in Benton County. They bought a little more land that joined their property. Every year something got a little better. There were a few more things you could buy if you had any money. They didn't hear from back home much. Grandpa's father, Charles Harpham, had died March 20, 1876 and was placed in Bairdstown Cemetery in Sullivan County, Missouri. His wife Ann had died September 22, 1869 and was placed in Bairdstown Cemetery also.

Charles Wesley's last child, Gladys, was born in 1899 in Edwards, Missouri. The rest of the family was getting older, dating, and getting married. By the early 1900s three of the oldest girls were married and Charles Wesley had two grandchildren.

By now times were sure getting better. Charles Wesley's family was getting quite a bit smaller. The old house was in bad shape. There were two rooms upstairs and two rooms downstairs with a drafty kitchen in the middle. There were a few sawmills around in the county by now. At this time Charles Wesley decided he wouldn't hew logs. He would get them sawed into boards. Most all saw mills back then were powered by steam engines. There still wasn't much money in the county. There weren't any chain saws. They used a two-man cross cut saw. My, if you owned one of them you were coming up in the world.

Well, anyway, he got several logs cut and hauled to the mill with horses and mules. When he got the lumber and logs sawed out, all of the neighbors came over and helped build the house. They called it a house-raising. For several years after this, all communities had house raisings when there was a burn out or disaster of some kind. Even when I was a kid they did a lot of house raisings and barn raisings. Now the government takes money from the working people to build billions and billions of houses, not only for the U.S.A., but all over the world. It seems to me such a waste. It would be better if neighbors helped take care of each other's problems. That is the way we used to do it and it worked really well.

By this time all of Charles Wesley's family was married and all still lived in Missouri. L.B. and Daisy Holmes lived at Hughesville, Missouri. They never had any children. They lived and worked on the farm for many years.

Bertha married W.C. Arnett on April 30, 1899. They lived their first seven years on the farm that was homesteaded by his father, William Henry Harrison Arnett. Later they bought the farm and several adjoining farms. In 1919, they built a nine room, two-story house. They spent their entire life on the farm where they raised livestock.

Jenny Harpham, the third child of Charles Wesley was married to Frank Buffon. They made their home in Benton County for a few years. In 1922 the Buffon's moved to Pettis County. They made a few more moves around there. In 1939 Frank and Jenny made their final move to Lamont, Missouri where they spent the rest of their life.

Gladys was the youngest of Charles Wesley's children. Her mother, Charlotte died when she was sixteen years old and she continued to live with her father, and brothers Elmer, and Roscoe in the two-room log house until she was twenty-three years old. She met and married John Rice. They lived in a house close to the

Bethel Church in 1923. From there they moved to LaMonte, Missouri. John worked as a day hand for other farmers. Later they moved to Cross Timbers, Missouri. Their final move was to Edwards where they lived the rest of their life. They raised four children. Gladys always liked nice things and enjoyed life. She was the first in her community to get her hair cut in a short style. She was very sociable, and she loved people and visiting.

Elmer was married in 1919 to Geneva Lyn Miller. They spent their first years at Kirksville, Missouri. They had four daughters. Elmer taught school throughout rural Missouri. He completed a master's in Administration at the University of Missouri. Elmer was Superintendent of Schools for many years. He believed in consolidation and building new buildings. Neva, his wife received a master's degree in nutrition from Vanderbilt University. They retired from teaching in Camdenton, Missouri.

My father was Roscoe Harpham. He met and married Grace Raymer. They made their home on the Harpham homestead farm. They lived on the farm all of their life. They raised four children. My father always farmed using a team and horse drawn equipment. He never owned a tractor. He was still hitching up the team and wagon every day when he was well into his nineties. My mother lived to be one hundred years old. She loved growing flowers and gardens. She was still tending her flowers well into her nineties. They were both blessed with a long and healthy life.

The following is a record of the events of my life from my childhood to the years of raising my family. I have recorded the details as I recall them.

# 1934

As a boy I grew up in Benton County. Times were hard and they got worse as the drought hit in 1934. It hung on for about three years. The winter of 1934, with the drought going on, was a dry winter. There was not much feed for the livestock. It was about two miles to school when we went. Lots of days we had to stay home and help with getting wood to heat the house and also to cook with. The wood had to be split real fine. Then it would cook good hot biscuits. It seems like biscuits were a lot better back then. Maybe it was just my taste. After we got the winter wood in and the corn out of the shocks we would get back in school for a few days.

We went to a one-room schoolhouse with a big jumbo wood stove in the center. Only one teacher taught all eight grades: reading, writing, arithmetic and the ABCs. After three or four weeks with our teacher we could figure square feet in a house, tell how many square feet of lumber in a log that was twelve feet long and two feet in diameter, and figure how much hay was in a round hay stack.

Well, the winter was still dry and cold so we had to start raking up acorns. We would put up four or five hogs to fatten out for our meat.

If there wasn't any corn, we would fatten the hogs out on acorns. The meat wouldn't be quite as good but it sure beat a snow bank. We always butchered our meat in wintertime so it would keep till we could get it smoked and sugar-cured. Then it would last all summer.

Butchering was a big thing back then. Several neighbors would meet at one farm to butcher everyone's hogs. We had big thirty or forty gallon iron kettles. We built a fire under them till we got the water hot. If you could dip your finger in it three times without getting burned, it was just right. We used big metal barrels. We set them on angles, put hot water in them, and then put the hog in. Then we would pull back and forth until the hair slipped. Next we changed ends with the hog. We would pull the hog out and put it on a low table. We scraped all the hair off.

It sure would be nice and white. Then the hog would be hung in a tree to gut out. After that it would be put on another table to be quartered and cut up. There would be several crews working so everyone would get their hogs butchered. Finally everyone would load their meat up and take it home.

    Most everyone had a smoke house. This was a place where you kept the meat. Usually there was a table in the middle of the building to lay the meat on. Then the drying and sugar-cure process started. Some farmers would smoke their meat. There were several ways you could keep the meat all year round. After it was sugar-cured and dried, you could wrap it in brown paper and put it in white flour sacks, any good white sack would do. This would keep flies out. Some of the neighbors would take big wooden barrels and put a two-inch layer of wood ashes in the bottom. Then they would lay two big hams on top of the ashes. They would pour on some more wood ashes till it was covered real well. They would do this until the barrel was full, making sure the wrapped packages of meat did not touch one another. When you were ready for meat you would take out one piece at a time. A knife and pliers could be used to pull a thin layer off the raw side of the meat, and then it was ready to cook and eat. It was really good.

After the butchering was all done it was back to school for a few days. We lived about two miles from the Antioch School. We got up and started doing chores with the lantern, cows to milk, then feed the team, and get them harnessed so they would be ready for a days work.

> We got up and started doing chores with the lantern, cows to milk, then feed the team, and get them harnessed so they would be ready for a days work.

There were always hogs to feed. We would plant a few oats for the milk cow and work team. During the winter months we would clear one acre of new ground for our cane patch. This is where we got our winter wood. We would keep the best wood over and let it dry. Then this was what mom cooked with.

# 1935

Well, the spring of 1935 was here. It was still dry and there were a few wild onions and wild garlic. There was not much grass. Back then we carried our lunch to school in a brown bag. There weren't any fast foods. Everyone had about the same kind of dinner which was usually a biscuit with meat of some kind and everyone had sorghum molasses. We would have one sandwich of molasses. It was really good. I always tried to have one meat sandwich so when we walked home I could pull some wild onions and put on my meat sandwich. It tasted really good. That would tide me over till I got home and got the chores done. We tried to get everything done by dark. There wasn't any electricity in those days. We never went anywhere at night. We were always tired and ready for bed after working from daylight to dark.

Come springtime each family had to work out their poll tax, which was a road tax. Dad would take the team. He would get one dollar and the team was worth one dollar.
If he took me along that was another fifty cents, so we could work our tax out in about a week. The work consisted of plowing out

ditches with the team and a twelve-inch plow. There wasn't any gravel very close so we would find a hillside that was gravelly.

We would plow it and then load it on wagons by hand. Good teams and high-wheeled wagons could haul about one yard of gravel at a time. We made our gravel bed for the wagon out of two-by-six boards. That way we could lift up one board at a time and dump all the gravel off on the road. Sometimes trees would fall across the road. We would take teams and drag them out of the way. There weren't any chain saws, so we used chopping axes, which we always kept sharp. It was a lot easier to cut wood with a sharp axe.

We raised almost everything we had to eat. Dad would take the team and wagon to town once a month. He would take wheat along and get it ground up for flour. The corn he would get ground into corn meal. About the only thing he bought at town was sugar, coffee, salt, pepper, and sometimes dad would get a nickel's worth of candy. That would be a big brown sack about two-thirds full. There were only a few kinds in those days, orange slices, chocolate thimbles, peanut clusters, or horehound candy. We didn't buy much of anything else. Maybe five gallons of kerosene for the lanterns and lamps, and then a few nails and steeples for fencing. It was about ten miles to town so it took all day to make the trip.

There were several little stores around. Jotem' Down Store, that's the store that when the storeowner didn't have what you needed, he would say, "I'll jot it down," so he could get it later. There was another little store pretty close.
It got the name of Smack Out. Every time you wanted something the owner would say, "I'm smack out," which is how it got its name.

Not too far away was another little store called Needmore. You can probably figure out how it got its name.

There was a train that came to Warsaw and if you needed a big thing or hardware, you would about always have to go to Warsaw. You had to have a pretty fast horse to make the trip in one day. It was about forty miles round trip. As the population grew in Benton County it became necessary for farmers to start freighting from Warsaw Depot to the southern part of Benton County. There was getting to be a few cars and a tractor now and then, but horsepower was still the prime source of farming and transportation.

Well, warm weather came and we were getting the garden planted and had put out all the crops. We always planted our corn when hickory leaves got as big as squirrel ears. It was still dry, not getting any spring rains. Our radio weather station still predicted rain, but no rain. Cows were out picking on the new grass, but it was not very big. It was starting to get pretty hot for this time of year. Crops were not growing good. Real hot weather was coming on way too soon. But the work went on anyway. We plowed the garden and fields every few days to try to use what little moisture we had. The old work team was beginning to get tender footed by now. We had to use them on the road everywhere we went as well as all the farm work.

As a young lad I always tried to do any kind of work that anyone else could do.

So I decided that I could put shoes on the old team. They were gentle and tired most of the time so they would let you pick up their feet. You could buy metal horseshoes of all sizes.

It only cost one dollar a horse to get your horse shod, but the problem was nobody had the dollar to spend. You would take a big hammer and bend the shoe to fit the horse's hooves. There were regular horseshoe nails to put the shoes on with. After a few rounds of that I got pretty good at it.

Anyway the old team was ready to go to town. It was time again to take the wheat to the mill for flour and corn to get ground into cornmeal. We would get a few months supply. Dad would get it home and mom would put it in lard cans or something to seal it up to keep insects out. By this time we were having some vegetables and things to eat out of the garden. It was still hot and dry. Things were still growing but not very good. We had already plowed the corn three times and it is not but about waist high. It should be about six feet high by now. It looked like maybe we would get a few roasting ears from the garden.

In drought time the insects get pretty bad. Grasshoppers were moving in. We always kept a few turkeys around to help keep the insects down. Every month it just kept getting worse. The turkeys ate so many grasshoppers they got sick. Most of our turkeys got blackhead so we had to doctor them for several months. Finally we had to pen them up.

It was getting into the fall of 1935. It was still very hot and dry in Benton County, Missouri. We were starting to put up some crops. Our hay was real short. We started cutting the hay with the old six-foot horse drawn mower. We had been sharpening up the sickle. We had an old crank-type grinding stone. It takes two people to operate it.

Anyway, the old sickle was sharpened and ready to go. First of the week we started haying. You can cut all day with a good team and horse mower and not mow more than four or five acres. Usually you had to let it lay and cure for a couple of days. But since hay was short and dried up we could put it up the next day. So we got an old dump rake out and started raking.

Then the whole family would get involved. After the field was raked we had what was called a bull rake. You put a horse on each end of this rake. The rake was fourteen feet six inches wide. You drove down the windrow until the rake got full. Then you pulled out of the windrow and headed for the haystack. Then back out from under the hay and go get another load. One or two guys would pitch the hay into a pile and one would do the stacking. This was an art to be able to put up a twelve-foot stack of hay that looked good and would turn water and keep good. This haying went on for a couple of months. The grasshoppers were still real bad. When we would get done haying at night we would stick our pitchfork handle back in the haystack to keep the grasshoppers from eating on them. They would eat a handle up if you left it out too many days.

After the hay was up we would start fencing the stacks so we could turn the cows in the meadow for the winter. We would feed the cows out of the haystack we built in the fall. With the haying done it was time to start harvesting corn and the other crops. The corn crop was way short, not much over waist-high and had only a few nubbins on it. This made the corn very hard to cut and shock.

The problem was the shock was wider than it was tall, so they wouldn't keep very well. We would try to haul it in early and put it in the barn.

We started on the cane patch after the corn was cut and shocked. Every year we would clean off one acre of woods seventy steps square, or two hundred and ten feet on each side. Cane always does better in the new ground that hasn't been farmed for a while. That's why sorghum was so good for people. It helped keep people healthy. The sorghum pitcher was on the table three times a day. People ate fat salty pork three meals a day. With no refrigerators, salted meat would keep all year round. Old timers believed if you worked hard every day and ate molasses three times a day you wouldn't have high cholesterol or blood pressure problems. If seemed to work. No one in my family had either and they lived to be in their nineties. My mother lived to be one hundred years old.

The next harvest was dry beans. We would pull the bean vines and take them to the yard where we would go to hulling them out. It took two or three hundred pounds to get us through the winter and spring. Mom and sister had been canning pickles all summer and still had a few late beets and cucumbers in the fall. Then we would pull the onions after they died and bent over. We would put them in big bundles and hang them in the smoke house, always leaving the tops bent over. They would keep all year but in winter we had to put them where they wouldn't freeze.

Next came potato-digging time. We needed six or seven hundred pounds to get through the year. We had to bury them. We would dig a hole in the ground where the water wouldn't run in.

We put a lot of straw down first. Then we would put all the potatoes in the hole and cover them with lots of straw and then put dirt on top. We also did the turnips and apples this way too. The two main buildings on our farm were the smoke house and cellar. Mom and my sister would can all summer. They would put the canned goods in the cellar to keep for winter. Things wouldn't freeze there.

Canning was a big job. It took about all of us. We three boys would help get the crops to the house and help get it ready to can. Mom and my sister, Ruth, did about all of the cooking and canning. Sometimes the boys would help tighten the lids. It took a lot of strength to do this. My brothers Charles Lee, Dean, and myself would have to keep good dry wood split real fine so mom could keep a good hot fire all the time.

Then there were ashes to carry out and jars of fruit to carry to the cellar and put on the shelf. We kept everything lined up, green beans in one place, peas, and the list goes on. There were vines from the beans and peas and we would take them to the barn hoping something would eat them and get some good out of them. There was never anything to throw away, no paper, no boxes, nothing to burn except wood. We didn't need any trash trucks to come by. There wasn't anything to haul off. Of course there wasn't any trucks in those days anyway.

It was getting late in the fall. We usually did a little fall plowing so we could put out wheat. This was important for us to get our flour for next year. We plowed about six or seven acres for planting wheat if we used the team of mules. They were what farmers called cotton mules, weighing about 1,000 pounds apiece.

They could pull a twelve-inch plow all day. You could only plow about one or two acres a day if you put in from daylight until dark. It took about a week to get it plowed, disked, and harrowed down ready for planting. By this time the weather was getting cooler. The flies and horseflies were pretty well gone. They were always bad in hot weather. So the livestock was getting some rest now.

We were starting to clean up another acre of ground for the next year's cane patch and get our winter wood. It took a lot of wood. The old house we lived in was made out of hand-hewed logs notched in the corners. Between the logs there were big cracks filled with clay. This was a two-room log cabin downstairs and two bedrooms upstairs, no heat upstairs in the wintertime. It sure was cold up there in the winter. The old logs weren't finished up. I believe you could have thrown a cat out the wall most anywhere.

In the winter we had big snows, so at night we would put our clothes under the bed to keep the snow from blowing in on them. The next morning we could hear mom say breakfast is ready, but she didn't hear us hit the floor because the snow pretty well cushioned the floor. Anyway it didn't take us long to get out from under the covers and get down to the old wood heater.

The old stove was always red hot to keep it warm inside the old log cabin. We would always draw a fresh bucket of water at night. We would set it by the old stove. Some mornings if it was too cold the dipper would be frozen to the bucket. We didn't have any thermometers, but we always knew if the dipper was froze, it would be really bad outside.

School is still going on at the old Antioch School. The old school was built like most other grade schools. Big wooden boxes about four feet long and thirty inches wide and eight inches deep were made. Some of the people would bring their teams and wagon and would haul gravel from the creek. Back then you could buy cement in eighty pound bags. Then some of the neighbors would bring  hoes and shovels. It took about eight to ten months to build the old Antioch School. It was made out of concrete. All the concrete was mixed and carried by hand in buckets and poured in the old oak frames, usually about 12 inches wide. It sure took a lot of material to fill those walls. If anyone had old pieces of metal like wagon wheels, tongues, or model T parts or frames, they would put them in the concrete walls to reinforce them. Then after it was built farmers started cutting logs and took them to the sawmill. When they were sawed up they loaded up the oak lumber on the wagons. Then they took it to the new school. Carpenters started their work. The wall was twelve inches wide so they would get two by twelve saw-outs at the mill to rough in the window openings. By this time you could buy some factory windows. All the framing was wood and the roofing was metal. The school was built to last forever. In fact there is still two of them standing within five miles of where I live.

There really weren't any carpenters, just farmers. Most everybody was knowledgeable about all kinds of work. Everyone learned to do everything. When the community would build a new school all the men and boys that lived in that community would donate their labor. Times were hard. You didn't hire anyone to do the work. You did it yourself.

Most of the old country schools were about alike, forty by twenty-four feet, usually four windows on each side and nothing on the back wall. Then the front always had double doors and it was a must to have the flue for the wood stove right in the middle of the school. There was always a big jumbo wood stove in every school. The old stoves sure took lots of wood to heat those old schools.

> Our teacher was a real good teacher. We called him the Walking Teacher of the Ozarks

Our teacher was a real good teacher. We called him the Walking Teacher of the

Ozarks. He walked about ten miles to school every day. He lived down by old Jordon, Missouri. He turned out to be the only teacher I had in grade school. At recess and noon he would get out and play games with us like softball, Flying Dutchman, and drop the handkerchief. Then Friday evenings we would have a spelling bee just for fun. It sure was hard to be a winner.

We didn't only have the Walking Teacher of the Ozarks, we also had the Walking Preacher of the Ozarks. This was a preacher that walked everywhere he went. He held revivals, would pastor a church, or just walk and preach everywhere he went. We sure could use some of that now-a-days. The Walking Preacher of the Ozarks held several revivals at the Antioch School through the years.

I remember another great man. He was very handicapped. He could hardly walk and had lots of other problems, but my how God used this man to do the Lord's work. I was young at this time and wasn't a Christian. I knew and everybody else knew that God was really using this man to help win the world to Christ. Every year there would be four or five revivals held at the old Antioch School.

They always held pie suppers or box suppers at the school too. This was a real big event. It wasn't only a fundraiser to help the community. It was a contest for the young unmarried girls to see if their pie would bring the most money. They would make up boxes to put their pie in and decorate it real pretty. It wasn't unusual for a pie to bring twenty-five to thirty dollars. The young boys would put their money together and try to buy the prettiest girl's pie. This was always a lot of fun. The problem was if you had a girlfriend and she took a pie, you could be sure the boys would put their money together to buy her pie. This always made the boyfriend mad. Sometimes there would be a big fight. Anyway it would help raise money for the community and was fun and entertaining too.

Back then there wasn't any electricity, TV, and not much radio. So we had to make all our entertainment for the community. The pie supper was held in the fall or winter and in the summer they would gather at the school and play ball softball, hardball, and lots of other games. The young kids had their own games like Flying Dutchman and drop the handkerchief.

Winter had come and gone.

# 1936

It was spring of 1936. It was still pretty dry, no rain. Livestock looked kind of bad, but everything made it through the winter okay. We built a log pen and put the old sow up. She was about ready to have pigs. Everyone just lets their hogs run loose most of the time. The old turkey hens were beginning to lay eggs. We had to find the turkey nests. Then when they would lay, we brought the eggs in and mom would put them under an old setting hen, usually a heavy breed of chicken. We would make nests in the hen house.

By gathering up the turkey eggs, the turkey would just keep on laying trying to get a nest full. Then she would set on them and hatch them out. So we would have plenty of turkey to eat and keep enough hens over to lay the next year. We always set old hens all during the summer months. That way we always had young chicken to cook year around.

It was time to start plowing. We would take the old white mule, Old Pete, and put him on the double shovel to start plowing our cane patch. This was always in new ground. It would be full of stumps and rocks. The first time it didn't do too good, but it would lay there, freeze and thaw, and then it would be the middle of summer before we would plant the cane.

By this time we were breaking ground for the other crops. Oats were usually planted last of February. Then we would plant corn. The other crops like soybeans and milo were planted. We would be planting the garden in between times. Mom always planted everything in their signs. We used to kid her and say, "Mom, why don't we just plant them in the ground." But what she did always worked. She would have a good garden if we got much rain, but it was still a drought in Benton County.

It was starting to get pretty hot and dry again. Most of the crops were coming up, but some would have to be replanted by hand. You would take a bucket of seed and a hoe, dig a hole, drop a seed in, and use your foot to cover it with dirt. You could plant a pretty big field in one day. We were starting to plow the corn for the first time with the tongue-less walking cultivator, which had wooden break pens. These would break if you hit a stump. You just stopped and whittled out another wooden pen and drove it in. Dad was talking about getting a riding cultivator for the next year.

School was still going on. We were getting to go most of the time now. Between times we would be helping the neighbors. Some of them had some bad luck. Their house burnt up, so all the neighbors around started cutting logs with hand crosscut saws.

Then the neighbors would take a load of logs to get them sawed and haul the lumber to where the house had burnt. When the lumber got there, we all pitched in and helped build the house back. Most people only had four rooms and a couple of rooms upstairs for bedrooms. With everyone working it only took about a month to build it, no wiring, no plumbing, no insulation, just oak boards on the inside and outside. Then they would put newspapers or building paper on the inside to keep wind and snow from blowing in. Nobody had any money or insurance. Everybody just helped one another in time of need. It was more like Bible times then.

Summer of 1936 came. It was sure hot and dry yet. The radio weatherman was talking about the drought might be coming to an end late that fall. We sure hoped so. The ground was dry and hard. Big cracks covered it. The ground we kept worked up was loose and dusty. We had been having some of those hot winds that go along with the drought. It had been above the one hundred degree mark off and on for several weeks. We were starting to put crops up. Mom got most of the canning done in the garden and a lot of fruit canned too.

The bean crop was short and several other crops were too. Dad, my brothers and I had set out about forty fruit trees a couple of years earlier. They were just starting to bear a little fruit. The hot dry weather was hard on them. We drew some water by hand out of the well and put around each tree. It sure was slow work. It seemed like we didn't get much done in a day. We still had a big woodpile left from last year, so we did not need to clear new ground this fall and winter.

We would probably use the old cane patch over the next year. Putting cane in new ground sure helped to kill out brush, stumps, and roots. The ground was plowing a lot better after the stumps and roots had rotted out. All you had to do then was go through and pick them up.

We liked to let the ground lay all winter. It freezes and thaws. It sure works better and is better ground next spring. We had been putting up hay again that fall. Same old story, the corn was about waist-high and short ears. Sure was hard to cut by hand. You just had to bend over all the time. It was sure hard on the back. We went through a little of the better corn and hand picked some of the best ears. We saved some for seed and the rest we would take to town and get ground for our winter cornmeal. If any corn was left we would feed it to the hogs to fatten out our meat. We always needed some for the chickens, turkeys, and the livestock. The heat had let up a lot. It was getting on into winter.

> Same old story, the corn was about waist-high and short ears. Sure was hard to cut by hand.

The radio weatherman was still talking about the drought being over by spring. Things were really bad. Most all the small banks and loan companies were going broke. Lots of farmers were losing their farms. Even if you owed less than one hundred dollars on your farm, you couldn't get any money to pay it off.

The government got involved by this time. It was so bad they began to buy up hogs and cattle and just dump them in the river to get rid of them. It did help out the fish. Going price for hogs around here was one dollar. Old sows and smaller hogs were fifty cents each. Pigs were about a quarter.

They would buy cattle too, three dollars for big cows, one dollar and fifty cents for yearlings and seventy-five cents for calves. Dad decided not to sell his for that little of money. It was an open winter since it was so dry. We got our livestock through in fair shape.

# 1937

  It was spring of 1937, and the radio weatherman was right. The drought was over. It started raining and the old earth was really soaking up that good water. There hadn't been very much run off yet. If it kept raining I was sure the branches would get up and run pretty big. Mom was so glad to have soft rainwater to wash the clothes in. She had been using the hard water and homemade lye soap. It didn't do very well. Mom always made homemade soap. She would cook down the skin of a hog. Then she added some lye to the rendered lard. This would make a large block of soap when it cooled. The large block would be cut up with a knife to make several smaller bars.

  Sure was nice to have water in the branches for the livestock again. Before, we drew all the water for everything out of the well by hand. It was a good well. Great grandpa had the well drilled with horses in the late 1800s. They drilled through a cave and water roared, running in for several days. Lots of neighbors didn't have that good of a well so they would drive cattle over here and draw water by hand for their herds. This went on all through the drought.

But now everyone was getting water in their branches and ponds. Well, things were sure looking better.

Most of the banks went broke during the hard times. Now they would loan a few dollars. Dad got several head of cattle through the winter. The demand for cattle was getting better. Cattle buyers were coming by on horse, wanting to buy the younger cattle.

Lots of the farmers in the lower part of Benton County, including dad, sold to the buyers that came by on horseback. There was one catch. We had to help drive them to Warsaw. There was a train that came there most all the time. The buyers and sellers got together and we started driving our cows toward Warsaw. The neighbor east of us brought their cows. This way we put our herd in with theirs. We picked up several herds before we got to Fristoe, Missouri on old 65 Highway. That was about ten miles. Then we headed north toward Warsaw. We picked up a lot more cattle between Fristoe and Warsaw, Missouri.

We had to drive cattle across the old swinging bridge. We could only let so many on at a time. Finally we got them across the river and over to the railroad cars. This was the biggest cattle drive I was ever on. Most everybody had to walk. There were a few horses on the drive and a few cow dogs.

It was about a twenty-five mile drive for most of the cattle. We let them stop and rest at night. When we got the cattle in the pens everyone got paid for their cattle. Dad sure did well. About six months before people were selling cows to the government for two or three dollars a head. Dad averaged about thirty-seven dollars and fifty cents a head for the cows he sold at Warsaw. That was the most money our family had ever had. We got us a bite to eat at the hotel and caught the mail hack and headed home. Some walked all the way. Others caught rides with people hauling freight out of Warsaw with team and wagon.

Times sure looked better. Grass was really growing. Crops were looking better that spring. It had been a little wet and we hadn't gotten everything planted yet. Mom's garden was really doing well. We were already having lettuce, onions, and a few radishes. We would be planting garden and crops all summer, since we were getting good rains. We had a few cows left at home. They had been having calves. They were sure doing well on the tall grass. We had a couple of new colts that year too. Most of our workhorses were getting older. So in about two years we would break out a new team and give the older horses a little more rest.

School was still going on. We had been getting to go most of the time. It would be out about the last of May. My Grandpa Charles Wesley told me a lot about what happened at the school and in this part of Benton County, Missouri. The old school was still in good shape for many years. It was the heart of the community. It was where people met if they needed to have a meeting about anything. There was no other community building of any kind, so they didn't just have school there. There were lots and lots of big revivals held at the school and lots of people accepted Christ into their life there.

> There were lots and lots of big revivals held at the school and lots of people accepted Christ into their life there.

The days were getting pretty long so we could get a lot of work done after school. Mom always had a treat for us when we got home from school. A big pan of hot light rolls with cow butter was usually waiting for us. We always got home on time if we could for the treat, but after that the work started. Some of us boys would go to the woodpile and split wood until dark. There was fence to fix, brush to cut, cows to milk, hogs to feed, plus chickens and turkeys to take care of and water to draw out of the well by hand.

Mom and my sister were usually canning or getting jars ready. They carried stuff out of the garden for the next day and then got supper ready. We all worked and worked hard and we all had a big appetite. We didn't have much of a variety. It was meat, potatoes, hot bread, and red-eyed gravy with some vegetables. Red-eyed gravy was made by adding a few tablespoons of coffee. There was no fast food in those days.

Well, it was still raining a lot. The old log house was starting to leak. It had wood shingles on it. Dad said we would have to cut and split out some wood shingles. We would pick out good white oak or read oak trees that sometimes would split real straight. Then we took the crosscut saw and cut off blocks about sixteen inches long. Then we split the blocks in half. We tried to split off half-inch slices from the block that would make our shingles. The roof was pretty steep so water would run off well without leaking.

Well, we got the old roof back in pretty good shape. There were times we would get a lot of hail, but hail usually didn't hurt those wood shingles. They were tough and the roof was pretty steep.

The year of 1937 had really been good so far. We were getting ready to mow the oats down for hay. That is the first part. That is what we fed the milk cows in the wintertime. They would milk well and the milk tasted real good. We would save about half of the oats and let it stand until fall. Then we would cut them with the horse binder. The binder would bundle them and then we would stack them and let them dry. About October we would have the thrashing machine come in and thrash them out. That would make part of our grain for the winter.

We used to cut and bind our wheat by hand, but now we used the horse binder to bundle it. We always tried to take good care of it. That was where we got our flour for cooking with each year. Crops were sure good this time. It looked like we would be able to fatten the hogs and cattle out on corn. We wouldn't have to pick up acorns to fatten them on. We would probably let the old sows run loose this winter. They would eat a lot of acorns. It looked like we could be able to keep all of the calf crop. The heifers would make good cows in about a year. This would build our herd back up again.

We were starting to hay the north forty. My, was it ever good, almost waist high. There would be stacks all over the forty acres. Dad bought a used six-foot cut horse mower. It was just like new. That sure helped on getting the hay cut. We would probably swap work with our neighbor to help get the hay up this time.

Dad said it looked like we would have to cut long poles to build a place to wean the calves in. We would try to build it pretty close to the water since we would have to carry it to the calves.

Then we would load up the hay wagon and bring up hay for the claves. The hogs were coming along good. It looked like they would weigh about four hundred pounds by butchering time. I was going to have to shoe the old work team. Dad needed to go to town in the wagon. Mom was getting low on flour and corn meal too. We were about out of coffee and sugar. We wouldn't buy much else but a little salt, pepper, and brown sugar. We used a lot of that when we butchered. I sure hoped dad wouldn't forget that nickels worth of candy. He had kind of spoiled us. Mom sure got a good job on hatching the turkeys and chickens this year, so we would have plenty of meat for the year.

The drought had been over several months now. Several good things were happening. The old team of mares had their colts. This would be a new team in a year or so. Since crops were good, mom and sis had gotten the cellar filled back up with canned fruit and vegetables. It looked good in there. They were all lined up in rows, beans all in a row and everything else lined up together. Also the field crops were all good. There were several big stacks of hay in the forty-acre meadow. Lots of big corn shocks in the field and the cane plants were really good, six or seven feet tall. This was the first time in three or four years that we had good crops. We were getting lots of rain and it looked like it might snow a lot that winter.

Well, by this time crops were about all in and the wood pretty well cut. We had a good cane patch. We cut and stripped it by hand. One of our neighbors had a cane mill. So we would load it up on the wagon and take it to the neighbor's mill about two miles north of us. We would stay all day and help make the molasses.

This would take several days. We had a lot more sorghum than we needed, so we would share with older people or anyone in need. That was the only way we survived was to help one another. There wasn't any handouts or welfare. We worked really hard for everything that we had.

We were back in school most of the time now. Weather was sure getting bad. We had already had one two-foot snow and lots of ice on the trees. When we went to school we would have to wrap our feet with gunnysacks to keep the deep snow from getting in our boots. The other problem was the heavy ice and snow on the trees. It bent them over in the road so we couldn't get through. This was sure a bad winter and a bad time to have to go to school. This went on about all winter.

# 1938-1939

January of 1938 was finally here. It was still cold and wet. We tried not to complain about the rain and snow after going through the drought for three years. We still had some big shocks of corn in the field. We took the team and wagon down there and knocked the snow and ice off of the corn shocks. We loaded it on the flat bed wagon. We did this about all winter. We fed this to the milk cows. We had to cut the ice in the branches for the livestock or draw water from the well by hand.

By March it had let up a little. Weather was getting better. It was starting to thaw out the ground. By the first of April it had really thawed out. It was so muddy the old high-wheeled wagon would cut down a foot or so. If you had to haul anything it really went down. All the old country roads got bad. The bottom just fell out of them. This meant that it was time for dad and all the neighbors to work out the road poll tax. As usual I helped and got fifty cents a day.

Well, by now the two colts we raised were big enough to work. They were pretty gentle so we didn't think it would be too bad. It was time for the planting season to start. We put the colts in with the old mares to work. It sure did lighten the load for the old team. By the time we got done planting the young team was working real good. We were still getting plenty of rain. Crops were coming up. Hay and pastures were looking good. Just about everything was better. There was getting to be a few cars and trucks around now. Also people were beginning to see a few tractors around. Things were starting to get more modern. That would give some of the old horses a little rest. Three of our neighbors went to Urbana to the Chevy dealers to buy three pick-ups. Two were 1938s and one was a 1939. If they would buy all three, they could get them for about six hundred dollars. That would take about six cows to buy a new truck. Today it would take about forty-five head of cows to buy one new truck. Seems like things are not quite right these days.

  Since times were getting better dad got one of the neighbors who had a steam engine and sawmill to come over and set up his mill. Dad, my older brother, and I started cutting saw logs. My younger brother wasn't old enough to help much. We started out selling oak fencing lumber, one by six full inches and whatever length they wanted. They were going to build a new school at Cross Timbers, Missouri, so dad got the contract on it to furnish all the oak lumber. He got about three dollars a hundred board foot delivered to school. We thought that was pretty good money back then. It wouldn't be much now.

Things were really booming around her. Banks were doing better. Some new ones were springing up here and there. Cross Timbers had three at one time. Cross Timbers had the biggest hardware and machinery store there was anywhere around. You could go out there and buy new Webber high-wheeled wagons, horse drawn plows, disk, mowers, a buggy, or just about anything you needed.

There was getting to be more cars and trucks on the road. There used to be all county roads. Now they were putting in some state roads. They had what was called the W.P.A.. This was a government project to help the poor. It started out to be a good thing but like many other government projects it got infested. Farmers all worked hard around here from daylight until dark. When the W.P.A. came out to work on new roads, they all stood around and leaned on their new government shovels. The old farmers called the W for we, P for piddle, and A for around. So they just called it the We Piddle Around program. They were building a new road here in front of our old homestead. This employed several teams and people.

> The old farmers called the W for we, P for piddle, and A for around. So they just called it the We Piddle Around program.

By this time dad was cutting logs for us a new home. My uncle was the head carpenter at Bagnell Dam. The work was over down there, so he started building our new house.

We put the old wood stove in it. Now, my uncle was an early riser. He always got up about 4:30 AM and built a big fire in the old wood stove. He would smoke the old pipe for about an hour.

By that time mom would have breakfast ready. She always had a big breakfast. We put up our own meat, had our own chicken eggs and always had the molasses pitcher on the table. That helped to counter act all that grease we ate all year long. Then we always had three big pans of hot biscuits with real cow butter. We always had lots of jellies. It was wild grape jelly or maybe tame grape jelly, plum and many other kinds. We always got everything there was that was good to eat.

We started out in the spring picking greens and lambs quarter, dock, mustard, poke, and a list of others. Then there was the garden stuff for canning. The early blackberries, dewberries, gooseberries, and blueberries were all getting good. Rhubarb and lots and lots of garden vegetables were ready too. My uncle had gotten the house way along by now. There was no electricity in this part of the country. He did everything with handsaws, hammers, wood chisels, planes, rasps, and hand routers. It was a slow process to build and finish a house like this. All the windows were routed out with a hand-held router. The walls were built with oak lumber, and by this time, you could get plaster. So he nailed old oak lathes on the wall. They were one and one-fourth inches thick and two inches wide. He nailed them on about three-eighths gap between them. This would hold the plaster on the wall.

The year of 1939 was about over. We had our crops about all up. Corn was shocked, hay was stacked, sorghum had been made, and garden vegetables were canned and put into the cellar. The potatoes and turnips were dug and buried. The cellar was pretty full. Mom and sis had canned lots of stuff.

Everything was lined up in order. It sure looked good. We had some apples and pears in there too.

Weather was pretty cold by now. It was time to butcher our hogs so we could have meat all year. Dad got the old metal barrel out and took the team and wagon and hauled in some firewood.

We had to draw the water out of the well by hand. This took several gallons. We also had to find some sort of pieces of heavy iron to put on the fire when the water got too cold to scald with. We would put the hot irons in the barrels to warm the water back up. Everything was together and ready. The neighbors all got ready to help butcher all the hogs. Sometimes there were too many to do in one day so we had to butcher the next day also.

The hard part of winter was about here, but we were pretty well ready. There was a lot of snow falling now. We were back in school part of the time. We always saved the old gunny sacks to wrap our legs in above our boots. The snow used to get real deep around here. School never shut down as long as anyone could get there.

# 1940

Spring of 1940 was a relief from the hard winter. One thing about the hard winter is that a hard freeze kills all the insects. The ground froze about two feet deep this winter. We probably wouldn't have too many insects that year. Maybe mom would have good luck with the turkeys. If they ate too many grasshoppers again they could get blackhead. Usually we had a good crop year after a hard winter. Dad was getting ground ready for the spring planting. I thought he was going to put out quite a bit more crops than usual. We were getting more cows this year. We had been keeping some of the heifers over so they were nice big cows by now. Sounded like he was putting out a lot more corn and might even rent some extra ground this time. We also needed more wheat, oats, and some extra hay.

We got the ground pretty well ready at home for planting. We would start on the rented land down on the creek. It was a little wetter so we might have to let it dry out a little more.

The creek had been getting up quite a bit that year. It even over flowed onto some of the plowed land. After several weeks of sunshine we could plant the low lands. We were kind of dreading the weeds in the corn. Wet weather would mean a lot of cockle burs, morning glories, horseweed, crab grass, and other weeds. When this happened the whole family would go down to the creek. Mom would take dinner. We all took our hoes. We would go row by row and hoe out all the weeds. We could do this while the ground was too wet to plow. We always used a walking cultivator, but I thought we were going to get a riding cultivator this time. That would make it a lot easier. It was several miles down to the leased land on the creek. It looked like we were going to have to put shoes on the old team and also the young team. The young team was harder to shoe than the old team.

We had been down on the creek several days. We had gotten it hoed and plowed out real good. Mom had come along and fixed dinner. Also she took the laundry. There was plenty of good creek water to wash clothes in. Dad would load the old iron kettle in and a little firewood. Sometimes mom would take time to catch some fish with the old cane pole. My, after hoeing corn until noon that made really good eating.

> Sometimes mom would take time to catch some fish with the old cane pole

It was still raining a lot. The creeks had been up and got all over the cornfield. I didn't think it had ruined it yet. We were still hoping for a good crop. The corn crop was pretty well laid by for now. Then we just waited to see what would happen.

We wouldn't be going back down there for a while. We might go a couple of times and take dinner while mom would be washing the clothes in the good creek water. Maybe we would even catch a few more fish.

Squirrels and coons were working on the corn pretty bad. We took the old two dollar and ninety-five cent Sears and Roebuck 22 single shot along. We could sure getem' with that. We were pretty sure we would have some meat for dinner too. We always took the big old iron skillet to fry in. Mom always had a gallon of hog lard along with potatoes to fry. If everything else failed she would take some eggs along to cook and a couple of loaves of homemade bread.

Winter was coming on again. The weatherman was predicting a good normal winter. We had been trying to get the corn crop off of the leased land before the creek got up and ruined it. The corn was pretty good. The coons and squirrels had eaten and destroyed a lot of the ears, but what was left was pretty good. Dad would grind the choice ears of corn up for corn meal. Then we could have good old hot corn bread and cow butter. You sure can't beat that. We would also have grain for the work team and cows. We had a pretty good oat crop. We saved a lot of that for the old milk cows. It sure did make the milk taste good. We stacked some of it and some we cut with the old horse binder. Then we could get it threshed. It was also real feed for the workhorses and the milk cows.

# 1941

My how time flies. It was now spring of 1941. The winter wasn't too bad. Livestock wintered pretty well. The ground began to thaw out. Dad wanted to start plowing. It took a long time to plow one acre with a team and twelve inch walking plow. It would take at least two months to get it all plowed if the weather stayed good. We got a few acres plowed last fall. We got one acre of timber cleared off for the cane patch. That made our winter wood for heating and for the cook stove all summer. There still wasn't any chain saws so we cut all those acres with good sharp chopping axes and cross cut saws. It took two men to use the saw. The next thing was to plow the acre of new ground for the cane patch. Since it was full of stumps all over we would take one horse and the single shovel and tear the ground up a little.

It had been a pretty good year so far. The old turkey hens had been laying and setting real good. It was always us boys job to get out and find the old turkey hens' nests.

This was always a lot of fun. The hens would start out one way to fool us. Then they would get out of sight. They would turn and run the other way to their nest. Sometimes they were hard to find.

If we found the nest we would take out some of the eggs and the hen would just keep on laying eggs trying to get a nest full to set on. Mom would put some turkey eggs under the old white rock chickens. They would set pretty well. It always looked funny to see an old chicken hen with eight or ten turkeys following her. She would be a good mother to them. Just like they were her very own chickens. The young turkeys fried up well, just like fried chicken.

It seemed like every Sunday we had company. Mom would say, "Boys, go catch me three fryers."

Now, these chickens were just running lose on the farm. So we made up some long poles with heavy wire on the end and a big hook. That way we could put it over their legs while they were running. This was always a lot of fun. We just made a game out of it. We had lots of first cousins living pretty close by. When the work was all done we would go to their house or they would come over to our house. There wasn't any TV and not much radio. We made up our own entertainment.

Sometimes that got exciting if the weather was warm and nice. We would go in the timber where there were hickory trees. We would pick out a tree the right size for however many boys there were. We all climbed the same tree. We all just went higher in the tree until the tree would bend over. When it got bent down to the ground everybody would turn lose but one and did he ever take a fast ride going through the air. Well, anyway it was fun and entertaining. We would do it again until everyone had gotten a fast ride. We all enjoyed the day with the neighbor kids and the cousins.

We always had a new game of some kind. The old wooden high-wheeled wagon was worn out and broken down. It had metal bands around the hubs to hold them together. We would take saws and cut the wood hub off so that we could get to the metal bands. Then we would find one of grandpa's Prince Albert tobacco cans and cut it one half into. That would make enough tin for two of our homemade hoops. We would cut down big sprouts, something about one inch in diameter and about three feet long. Then we nailed the Prince Albert can on the end of a stick. Next we bent it to fit the size of ring we had. Then the fun would start. We would start it rolling with the stick which had the tin can nailed onto it. This was what guided the wheel. We played the game to see who could run the fastest with it and jump logs, big rocks, or anything else. It was really a fun game. We could entertain ourselves for hours.

We had all kinds of homemade games that we made ourselves. There wasn't any to buy so we just made our own. Another one that got exciting was to go into the timber and find small trees about one and one-half inches in diameter with a limb in the right place. We would cut the tree about two feet below the limb. Then we let the limb stick out about six inches and cut it off. Then the stick would be about six feet long. We would get up on them and walk around. We would get pretty good at it. That put you up to almost two feet off the ground. We would try to run over rocks, but nobody went too fast.

There were several other games we played. We were always making a cart to ride on. You could take an old cultivator wheel and put a wooden axle under it. Then you would add a coupling pole, a piece of wood that went from the front axle to the back axle. We'd sit on the coupling pole and put our feet on the front axle to guide it. Then we would find a big hill to go down. There weren't any brakes, so sometimes we went pretty fast. When we would get to the bottom everyone helped roll the cart back up the hill. Then someone else got to ride. This was a lot of fun. We could put in all evening doing this.

Sometimes we would play Flying Dutchman, drop the handkerchief, paint the double shovel, leap frog, marbles, and a number of other games. We would even break some of the young horses to ride. If that was not enough, we would ride some of the calves. We never got bored. There was always something to do. This sure kept us out of trouble.

Well, the fun was about over for a while. We had lots of work coming on. It was just another regular season with plenty of good rain. Crops all looked good. We had been back to school some. We got an old battery radio that we turned on sometimes to get the world news. It seemed like things didn't sound too good.

But the old U.S.A. seemed to be in good shape. There were a lot of problems overseas.

So much for the bad stuff now. Benton County was in good shape. The weather had been nice all summer and was still pretty good this fall. We had to stay out of school some to get the crops done. We had to get the sorghum made before it froze too much. That would take all of us a couple of weeks to get it all made and put up.

By then it was December 1941. We turned on the radio for about fifteen minutes to get the world news and we were given more news than what we wanted to hear.

The Japanese had just bombed Pearl Harbor. My, what a mess! People dead all over the place, big ships had been sunk, docks all destroyed and buildings and houses destroyed. They kept finding more dead people. It sounded like a few hours later the Air Force had gotten ready and run the Japanese back home. This news was the beginning of World War II for the United States. They drafted thousands and thousands of soldiers. This was real war. It turned out to be the biggest war we had ever had to fight.

At this time my brother and I were too young to be drafted, but it got a lot of our cousins and neighbors. Things just weren't the same around home any more. The government had started rationing almost everything and they began sending it overseas for the war effort. You just couldn't buy sugar, coffee, salt, and hardly anything to eat. It sure was a good thing for us that it was a good year for crops. Mom got up a good supply of garden stuff. We had good big hogs to butcher. Apples and peaches were pretty good this time.

All of the fruits and berries were good. We got lots of wild grapes, which sure made good jelly. The wild gooseberries were good too. Wild huckleberries had been good this year. The hazel nuts, walnuts, and hickory nuts were good also.

# 1942

It looked like we would be able to make it till spring of 1942. Kerosene for our lamps had been rationed and so had gasoline, tires, and all kinds of machinery. The war really sounded bad. They were still drafting a lot of people for the war. My older brother was going to be old enough before long. Already so many boys in Benton County had been drafted that there was not enough people left to get the farm work done. Some families got hit a lot harder than others. It looked like we would be too. It was looking like a bad year for most families. Their boys were being drafted. Several of them had already been killed. Lots of them were in the service and there was not much help at home to get the work done.

My older brother had been drafted and sent to Camp Chaffee, Arkansas for service. I think there were about fifty drafted out of Benton County, Missouri. So dad would be short one helper in getting crops out and harvesting them. The neighbors would all get together and help one another. It seemed like they were still getting crops planted okay.

> I think there were about fifty drafted out of Benton County, Missouri.

Probably they wouldn't get the corn plowed as many times this year. We usually plowed the corn four times and had the weeds pulled out when they were about knee high. Then in the fall if the weeds got too big we would pull them out again.

We got a letter now and then from my older brother. He had been in Camp Chaffee a long time, but it sounded like his whole company would be moved out before long. They didn't know where they would go this time.

# 1943-1944

Well, it was 1943 by now and it looked like I would be drafted before long. I was in high school and still helping dad at home all I could. Sure enough one day I got this card in the mail. It said, "Greetings, You have been drafted. Report to the courthouse." The card was signed by a government official.

Well, the day came. I had to quit school. We lived about twenty-five miles out of Warsaw. There wasn't any transportation except horse and buggy, horseback, or walking. I got ready to go. I walked several miles, then caught the mail hack and got to ride the rest of the way. We had to be there by 10:00 AM. I just barely made it.

Anyway we all gathered on the Benton County Courthouse yard. There were about thirty-five of us at this time. They assigned us a captain for our team. My, he was a great big guy. He would be our leader until we got to where we were going.

We got ready to go on the train. Then we got the bad news. The leader said, "Some of you guys will be going to Camp Sibert, Alabama for chemical warfare training." What a dreaded place this was. We went to Jefferson Barrack. Then we were split up again. I got the bad news again. I would be in the bunch that would go to the chemical warfare testing field. I was just a kid, never been too far from Benton County. Anyway we rode another train and got to Attala, Alabama. We were picked up in big 6 X 6 army trucks and then hauled to Camp Sibert, Alabama.

> We got ready to go on the train. Then we got the bad news.

We got there in the evening. They issued us our clothes, gas masks, and lectured us hard for about two hours. Then they assigned us our tent, which would be our permanent home as long as we were at Camp Sibert. There were about four hundred people that had been drafted for the 96 Chemical Warfare Company. There were people from all over the U.S.A, from the east coast to the west coast, and from Texas to Chicago. There were lots of tough guys in there and several of us kids that had never been away from home. The next morning they blew the whistle. We all fell out and lined up. They put us in four platoons.

Day number two had come and we lined up again. We were marched all the way down to this big testing station. It was a big unit that was built airtight, so they could release chemicals in there such as mustard agent, mustard, lewisite, and more. They started us on smaller doses. We usually stayed in the station one and one-half hours. It wasn't too bad the first week, but they just kept on making it stronger every week. Sometimes we would use an old worn out leaky gas mask and protective clothing and sometimes we didn't have anything to protect us.

As the weeks went on it really got bad. You would get claustrophobia and almost go crazy. It got so bad the soldiers would run out sometimes. Finally they put guards at the door with billy clubs and pistols. Nobody ran out then. You either had to stay or die. This chemical testing was not only in the station, it consisted of lots of field training, smoke screening and small arms chemical training. The government leased 35,000 plus acres to do this dirty training on. Most every day was just about alike, one and one-half hours in the station and one and one-half hours marching with full field pack, one hour in smoke screen, two hours on rifle field, three hours going through the infiltration course and then we would just march another three or four hours or until night. The rifle training consisted of rifle chemical training. They had long lines of telephone poles lined up lying on the ground, probably one fourth of a mile long. Then you would put this chemical grenade on the end of the guns. This would put the butt end of the gun on the pole. It kicked so much you couldn't hold it on your shoulder.

In field training we had big walls to climb over. Then they used big rope netting like they used on ships. We would climb to the top and back with the full field pack.

Next there was the crossing the creek of water. They had one and one-half iron pipe up over the water. You had to cross it by hand holding on to the iron pipe, one hand at a time. Lots of the guys didn't make it. They fell into the water. It didn't make any difference to the army if the water was real cold.

Their theory was that it would make you tough. Then there were push-ups with full pack. Boy was that ever hard to do.

We had trained for about three months and the training got harder and harder every week. It looked like we would be shipped out in a couple of weeks, but they hadn't let up a bit on the training. We got more real bad situations to go through. This time it was a different kind of firing range. We marched about twenty miles to get to the field. This was a huge place. At one end of the field they had several rifles set up stationary and some big guns. They would shoot level about three feet above the ground with some real ammunition and some tracer ammunition so that you could see it was the real thing. We had to get ready with guns and a full field pack. Then we had to crawl on the ground and try not to get up or you knew you would be shot. This was about one-fourth mile. It took about forty-five minutes if you were fast. At the end was a big trench full of water.

Now when we would all get there we would have to line up again. We would start the long march back to camp. This would take about three and one-half hours. Our clothes were wet and full of dirt and sand. It would rub you raw between your legs and under your arms and even in your feet. It seemed like the worst the army could treat us the better they liked it. Their answer was always, "This makes you tough."

It looked like training here at Camp Sibert was about over. We would be around the camp a few more days and then we would get a furlough before we were shipped out. Sure enough the next morning we got a fourteen-day leave.

I caught the train out of Attala, Alabama and headed home. Back then the train stopped at every little town, picked up egg cases, ten gallon of cows milk and people. I thought I would never get home.

After three days on the train I got home. My, was that ever a great moment. Just to see all my family. My older brother was still in the army. Well, we were having a good time. There were lots of big meals. Mom invited all my cousins and friends over several times. After being drafted into the army, you really appreciated home. You know we take a lot for granted. This had been the best time in my whole life so far.

My leave was running out and I had to catch the mail hack the next day and head back to Camp Sibert, Alabama. I would probably have to walk part of the way to Warsaw. Not too many cars were around yet. I finally got to the train depot and started the long slow journey back to camp. It would take about three days time. It made all those stops again.

We finally got back to Attala, Alabama. Then there would be big 6 X 6 trucks there to pick us up. There were about four hundred soldiers coming back to camp from all over the U.S.A. We had been given orders the next day that we would be shipped to California and from there, somewhere overseas. It took about one week to get packed, paperwork done, and everything ready. There were four hundred of us, so we got a special train to carry us to California.

After a few days in California we found out we would be sent to Guadalcanal as the 96$^{th}$ Chemical Warfare Company and that we would be the chemical depot where all the chemicals and ammunition and lots of other supplies would come through. From there they would be sent to the front lines.

We finally got on the big troop ship that was headed for the South Pacific. It was almost everyone's first trip on a big ship. After a day or two we began to get seasick. That big of a ship just rocks and rolls and bounces all of the time. The ocean seemed to be rough all the time. We would go down to the cafeteria in the bottom of the ship. My, everyone was seasick. Vomit was so deep you couldn't stand up and the smell was really, really bad. Nobody ate much for days.

The only thing you could see was water. Sea gulls would follow us all the time. You wondered how they lived out there with no land or place to light on. We saw a big fish and big whales. Some looked to be twenty to thirty feet long. The birds, fish, and whales followed the ship to eat the garbage and sewage that came out of the ship.

> You wondered how they lived out there with no land or place to light on.

We had been on the ship quite a while. We would be crossing the equator before long. The army made a big deal out of that. Every soldier was initiated and that was pretty rough treatment. I guess it was fun for the ones that were doing it but it wasn't much fun for me.

We had been on the ship a long time now. We had run into a storm over the ocean, so it would take several days to go around it. We got pretty close to Australia. We could see land and did that ever look good. We kind of went around it.

We could see a big bunch of sheep grazing on the grassland. That sure looked good to see some livestock. Anyway, the storm let up. Sea gulls were still following us. The big whales and big fish were still jumping. We were heading back in where you couldn't see anything but ocean water. We were headed for one of the little islands.

This would take another four or five days to get there. We had been on the ocean now about two weeks. We soldiers were getting over our sea- sickness a little at a time. You could go down to eat now and there wouldn't be vomit all over the floor. We had never hit any smooth water since we had been on the ship. The ship rolled constantly. Even when the ocean was finally calm the waves would go over the top of the thirty foot ship.

A few more days had gone by. We might get to see some land in the next couple of days. It had been kind of cloudy out here all the way. We hadn't seen a lot of sun. We got up early the next day and went out on deck. It looked like some mountains coming in sight. Sure enough by night we made it to a little island in the South Pacific Ocean. We would be around here for a few days unloading, packing, and loading things out to go up to the front lines.

We were told there would be smaller ships, boats, and barges to take us to Guadalcanal. Sure enough after two or three days, we got this small vessel loaded up. It was going to Guadalcanal. About fifteen of us got this old open top LST that had been in a lot of bad battles. It was shot up, bent up, and had holes in it.

We started out to Guadalcanal. They gave us several buckets to dip water out of the old boat. They said if you want to make it to the other island you will have to dip a lot of water to keep the old boat from sinking. I didn't think we were going to make it. We had to dip water day and night. Anyway, after a few days of dipping water we finally got in sight of Guadalcanal. The closer we got the more we could see the main beachhead and big battlefield. We could see all kinds of big ships sticking up out of the water.

There were at least fifteen or twenty big vessels sticking out of the water. It sure looked bad to pull into a place like this. There were several Japanese snipers still on the island. You had to be careful not to run into a sniper.

All four hundred of the 96th Chemical Depot Company was coming in on different kinds of ships. The Japanese Army had moved to another island. We still had a lot of Japanese snipers, land mines, bombs and wild hogs to beware of. The quartermaster post was already in place. We began to set up tents. They would hold five soldiers. They were just a place to sleep. We were on guard duty or working to get things set up for the 96th Chemical Company.

We had been on the island for about a week. We had gotten most of the things set up. We had a big long tent for the mess hall. It must have been two hundred feet long, but when four hundred people got in there at one time, it was too full.

The meals were pretty much the same everyday. Breakfast consisted of gravy with some kind of ground meat cooked in it. In order to be served we had to stand in the serving line with our mess kit. They would slop the food all over the mess kit that we used for a plate. Usually we got some kind of bread.

The dinner meal was cooked in those big thirty-gallon pots. All of our food was shipped over dry in cans, usually stew or goulash for dinner with crackers, coffee, or water. We had to purify all our drinking water. It came out of the ocean. Some days we would get lucky and get good old navy beans. That was a treat. Occasionally we would get real potatoes. Then the evening meal would be whatever was left over from the other meals. The meals were always cooked in the big thirty-gallon containers.

> We had to purify all our drinking water. It came out of the ocean.

There was always K.P. duty. Usually that took fifteen to twenty guys. When we had real potatoes we would hand peel at least four hundred pound. That sure took a lot of peeling.

There were lots of gallon cans and boxes to open to feed four hundred soldiers. Whatever it was, it took a lot of it.

After we got done eating, we washed our own mess kits. There was a one thousand gallon water tank on a five-foot stand to get the water out of for washing the dishes. They had several big vats of hot water. There was one for you to get the food off in, a washing vat, and then one to rinse with. You always had disinfectant in the dishwater. When a soldier got through washing their gear then those on K.P. duty would start cleaning up the temporary kitchen. All those big pots had to be washed and then we would carry out the garbage. We took it out a long way from the camp and fed it to the wildlife.

We had to be careful about getting it too close to the camp. The wild hogs would come in at night and tear up our food for the next day. We did guard duty or K.P. duty pretty often.

After we got the Chemical Depot set up way out in the jungle, seven of us were moved out there to guard, repair, and unload chemical coming in and also load chemicals going out. We didn't only have chemicals, we had all the ammo that the army used and any other explosives too. That was why we had to guard the dump twenty-four hours a day.

There were still a lot of Japanese snipers around. The wild hogs were destructive too. The longer the war went on the more repair work there was to do to keep the boxes and cylinders in good shape. The dump was way out in the jungle in a big canyon with high hills on three sides, quite a ways from anything else. This helped to protect it.

There was only one-way in and out. It took big 6 X 6 all wheel drive trucks to get in and out there. We would rotate guard duty. Then we could all get a little sleep. It seemed like every week it got worse out there. More leaky cylinders and more boxes tore up to fix. It was a dread everyday to do this kind of work. You got up in the morning when the sun began to come up. We camped on top of the hills around the dump. It would look gray and hazy down in the valley where the chemicals were leaking and the air smelled bad. I was left hostage in this condition all the time I was on Guadalcanal, almost three years.

There was no water at the dump. We would haul drinking water and canned food out from the 96th Chemical Company kitchen. Our meals were whatever we could get out of a can or box. We didn't have any kitchen so we would open up a 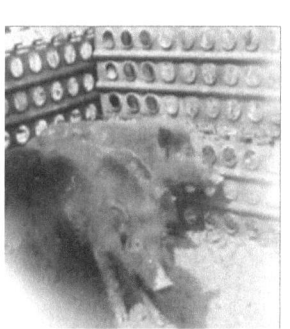 box of something or a can of whatever there was.

There was a hill on the other side of our tent. We could throw the empty cans in a big canyon over the hill. The wild hogs came in at night rattling through cans trying to get something to eat. It kept you on edge. You didn't know whether it was Japanese snipers or wild hogs. Well, anyway that would make cold chills run up your spine. These wild hogs had real long noses. They could eat out of a small can.

It had been one year since we came and things still were not getting any better. War was really bad on up front. It was sure taking a lot of ammo up there. Several big loads were going in and out every week. There was no electricity out where we were. We finally got an old battery radio. We got a little news now and then. Back at camp the 96th Chemical Company had gotten some generators so they had electricity part of the time.

There was some fruit on the island. Once in a while I could get one hour off and I would get an old weapons carrier and go up in the mountain a little way. You could get several big stalks of bananas and papayas. The bananas grew on big stalks. We had to bring the whole stalk in and put it in a dry dark place to let the bananas ripen. The native people kept all the ripe ones pulled, so we had to get ours green and let them ripen. This was a real treat after eating out of cans and boxes for so long.

# 1945

It was getting into 1945. Everything was in a regular routine loading and unloading chemicals and ammunition. The 96th Chemical Company really needed some ice to help keep food. Since I was mechanical minded and had helped build lots of things they called me in to the Chemical Company and there the mechanic, welder, engineer, and anyone that knew much about building began building.

We all agreed that there was a need for a big iron box. This box or tank should be at least twenty feet x twenty feet and four feet high, with a metal top on it. Then we could cut a square hole in the top about four and one-half inches by thirty inches.

We had a vehicle salvage yard, a boat salvage yard, and a real big airplane salvage yard. We had a lot of used stuff to work with. Old boats and ships had big flat pieces of metal in them so we used a piece of that for the square tank to hold the water.

Then the next step was to take a jeep motor and transmission to set in front of the tank. We had to fix a shaft so we could put a boat propeller on it. This shaft had to have a seal that wouldn't let the water out while the jeep was running and turning the propeller. We got that all fixed.

The next step was to make wedge shaped trays that would hold water. We took flat iron and made it fit in the holes. We cut in top of the tank. These trays were four and one-half x thirty inches x thirty-six inches deep. They would stick down in the tank that was full of water and salt. We knew that we needed lots of salt in the tank.

Then it had to be circulated in a pretty fast motion. We were ready to experiment to see if it would really work. The tank was full of water with lots of salt added to make brine. The trays were filled with good clean water. We started the jeep motor, put it in gear, and then started the propeller turning. The tank water was moving real well. We just needed to wait now and see if it would work. We weren't sure how much salt we would need or how long it would take to make the ice.

After several hours it hadn't froze very well, so we put in some more salt. In a couple of hours it began to freeze, so we decided we needed a little more salt. That really helped.

We built some wooden boxes to put one tray of ice in. Every tent of five would get one tray of ice everyday. Sure enough we emptied all the ice out and everyone got ice. It sure did help to have something cold to drink for a change. It was really hot over there.

The trays were made tapered so that when you lifted them out of the tank and set them in the sun for a few minutes they would slide right out. The kitchen got ice and we got to take some ice back to the tent at the ammo dump.

Things had been okay at the chemical dump. We always had a lot of work to do. There were several torn up and cracked boxes and cylinders plus the loading out of more ammo. Sometimes we had fighter planes or helicopters fly over while loading and unloading on boats.

There was a big boat coming in loaded to the brim with all kinds of ammo and chemical ammo, plus lots of other explosives. It docked in late one evening. It was too late to unload at night. It was about 10 PM at night. Two of us had just got up to the tent on top of the hill at the dump. We got in our army cots. This was a five-man tent. The cots were about four and one-half feet apart. We had mosquito nets over our cots. Mosquitoes were really bad out there. The ocean was a real good place for them to breed and hatch.

Anyway we just got in our cots to get a little rest and we heard the biggest blast I had ever heard. The whole island was shaking and moving in a matter of seconds. Here was this melted piece of hot metal about four feet wide and three feet thick and red-hot crashing down right between our cots. It burnt a big hole in our tent and if it had been six inches either way it would have killed one of us. This big pile of red-hot metal stayed red for two hours or so. We tried to move our cots and stuff out of the tent so they would not catch on fire.

> The whole island was shaking and moving in a matter of seconds.

We were still in shock all night. The guys guarding the dump thought the Japanese had blown up the dump. We were all scared to death. There was not any sleep the rest of the night.

Finally daylight came. We found out all about how the Japanese came in and blew up this huge cargo ship. There was hardly anything left of it.

Day two after the ship blew up we took the old weapons carrier into the Chemical Company and then went to the quartermaster to get a new tent. It had just ruined the old tent. While we were there we also picked up some canned goods too and anything else that would keep. It sure does get old eating out of cans or sea rations all the time. We were lucky we got enough to survive on. That was a plus. While we were there we also picked up about one hundred pounds of ice. My, that really helped to have cold water to drink. All we got was ocean water that had been processed and chlorinated. When it was hot it did not taste very good. But when we put ice in it, it sure made it a lot better.

We went down to the ocean to help unload another ship that had come in. There were dead fish lying everywhere and had washed up on the shore. There were some of the biggest fish I had ever seen. There were sharks and every kind of fish there is in the South Pacific Islands. The odor was really getting bad. They had gotten backhoes down there and were raking the big fish out and burying them to get rid of the odor. This took a day or two. There were thousands of them to be buried and gotten rid of. We were hoping the next day we would be able to get out of there and get away from the smell of dead fish and chemicals.

Back at camp, the cylinders seemed to leak most of the time. Things were back to normal. We still had to really guard the dump. The Japanese would sure like to blow it up. I was going to take time to go back up in the mountains and get some more fresh fruit. We had been out there for a long time. The banana crop was real good that year. Papayas were good too. We got a pretty good truckload. This would last a few weeks longer.

By now the Japanese had thinned out a little. One of the posts of the army was going to do some truck farming around the island. There was two acres of good flat land with good black dirt. The army got in some farm equipment, a tractor, plow, disk, planter, cultivator, and about everything you need to farm with.

Now they had gotten their seed in. This consisted of corn for roasting ears, potatoes, green beans, dry beans, tomatoes, cabbage, lettuce, beets, greens, peas, and cucumbers. Just about anything would grow there.

They got them all planted. It rained about every day or two so the crops really grew. They had already been cultivating some of the crops like corn and beans. They were going to plant watermelon, cantaloupes, and pumpkins a little later on. My, the crops were coming on good. The corn had been cultivated for the last time.

This meant the Chemical Company would get to have some of the fresh vegetables. We wouldn't have any at the dump. There wasn't any place to cook out there. Well, anyway this would be a big treat for most of the Chemical Company and the other companies too. We were hoping that when the watermelons got ripe, maybe we could get a few now and then.

The natives got in the garden crops pretty bad. You couldn't blame them. They had never had anything like this. The army was going to train the natives how to grow vegetables and garden stuff.

The native women do about all of the work. They would probably have to train the native women instead of the men. They won't get to take over the gardens until the war was over. It looked as if that was going to be a long way off.

Most of the native men didn't do anything only sit around and eat coconuts. They climbed trees to help shake the coconuts off. You had to be careful about walking under a coconut tree because the coconuts would fall off the tree when they got to a certain stage. Lots of these coconut trees were forty or fifty feet tall. The coconuts weighed about four or five pounds apiece. They really hurt, and if they hit you on top of the head it would probably have killed you.

The coconuts had a real hard hull to get off. The natives could get it off real easy. The American soldiers had to work at it to get it off. When you got the hull off, then there was a place on the nut you could make a hole in it and drink the coconut milk out of it. This was what the natives did most of the time. Well so much for that. Just remember, don't walk under a coconut tree. You might get killed.

There was some wildlife on the island and lots of wild hogs. There were lots of fruits and berries. The natives didn't work or put up any food. It just seemed like God took care of them. I guess that is why they live so long, no worries or stress. Just good, easy going times.

We had to be careful and not damage any of the coconut trees since this was their livelihood. The government had to pay so much a tree if we did damage one.

Most of the animals came from Australia. They grew lots of sheep, goats, and other animals and crops. Most of the meat we got was in cans from Australia. They called some of it corn beef and cabbage. I don't know what was really in it. When you opened up the square can, it spewed out and blew gas for quite a while. It had a real bad odor to it. When the smell got away and the gas was gone you could kind of eat some of it. It sure did stick to your ribs. You didn't get hungry for several hours.

We'll it seemed like war was getting better. We were not quite as busy as we were. We needed a break out here. We were all about to go crazy being held hostage in this dreaded place. The chemicals and mustard agents worked on your nervous system pretty hard. There was hardly anything you could do to help get rid of the stress.

My, we had gotten up one morning and got the word that war was over. They said they had bombed Hiroshima and Nagasaki, raised the flag, and the Japanese had surrendered. What a relief. No more ammunition coming in and none going out. We wouldn't have to guard the ammunition dump all the time now.

The snipers had let up and most had gone home except a few who hadn't heard that the war was over. Things would be different out here. We could relax a little. Some of us were going to take the old weapons carrier. It was a 4 x 4 with big tires pretty high off the ground. It would go about anywhere. There were a lot of pretty sites on the island that the Japanese hadn't shot up. We got out quite a ways from the dump. There was a little creek with not much water in it so we crossed it and went to the other side. It sure was pretty over in there.

It started raining so we decided we had better head back. We always carried our rain suit. One minute the sun would be out and then it might rain hard for three hours. The soil was pretty sandy along the ocean. When it quit raining the water would go right into the ground. This was what happened when we were on the other side of the river. It just rained and rained for about three hours. We finally got back to the creek and it was really getting big. We couldn't cross it. So we knew we would have to stay all night.

The rain had quit, the creek was roaring, and we didn't have anything to eat with us except roasting ears of corn we had picked up at the $96^{th}$ Chemical Company before we left. We built us a fire on the ground and put in some of the ears of corn with the shucks still on them. We put a little dirt around the outside of the fire and kind of made an oven to keep the corn cooking. It took about two hours to cook it this way.

Finally it got done, so we started eating the roasting ears. Boy, were they ever good or maybe we were just really hungry. Anyway this tided us over till morning.

After a rough night with no bed and no tent, we were up early. The creek was down so we could cross it. It took quite a while to get back to the dump. The guys wondered what had happened to us. Well, it got rid of a little stress. The confinement and chemical working conditions had driven us all crazy for the last three years.

Things were sure changing at the main headquarters. They would send one company back to the U.S.A. at a time. It took a big troop ship to do this. It would take several weeks to get the ships in and get all the companies out. There were several big companies still on the island. The Quartermaster and Motor Pool along with the 96th Chemical Company would be here a while longer.

# 1946

Since war was over we didn't have much to do. The guys from Maine and I decided we needed to do something to clear our minds. There were lots of real big butterflies over there. We went to the old airplane dump or salvage yard where all the old shot down planes were. In the wings of some of these planes there were long pieces of tubing. So we got several pieces of tubing that would telescope. They were in twenty-foot sections. We could telescope them out real long, forty or fifty feet.

Then we found some one-fourth inch rods.

We bent that in a circle and fastened one to one end of the pole. Then we got some old mosquito nets that had been on old bunks. We took a big piece of this and fastened it around the hoop and made it into a cone shape. We were ready to catch butterflies.

Now most people might think you were crazy when you chase butterflies. That was close to right. We were just one step away from that after what we had been through. Well, anyway this was going to be our hobby over here. The big butterflies flew pretty slow and pretty close to the ground. This made it a whole lot easier to catch them.

Our first trip out we did pretty well. We got four or five apiece. We would telescope the rod out, scoop up the butterfly, and turn the rod one-half over. This would keep the butterfly from getting away until we could let the pole down and take him out to put in a box.

The next day we went over to the medical place. We told them we needed a needle and some formaldehyde to preserve some butterflies. They sure had funny looks on their faces. They just knew we had lost our minds and gone crazy. We had a lot of explaining to do. We explained that this was going to be our hobby so we wouldn't go crazy. Finally they gave us the needle and formaldehyde.

We got a big piece of cardboard and several straight pins.

We would pin the butterflies on the board with the wings straight across so they would look good. Then we shot them with formaldehyde. This made them stiff and would preserve them for life. I caught them in 1946 and they are still good. I believe they will out last me quite a bit.

This turned out to be a good hobby. While all the other companies were moving out, we were going to have some spare time. The pressure was really on. We wanted to go home. We just kept on hunting butterflies. This would relieve a lot of pressure. By this time I had caught over one hundred butterflies, but a lot of them were not good enough to keep. Some would have torn places on their wings or something else was wrong. They were sure worried about us chasing butterflies. We weren't over the hill yet, just close to the edge.

Well it was time now to start making the trays to put them in. There was a lot of pretty good wood working shops on the island that hadn't been torn down yet. There were several different kinds of native wood here too. There was rosewood, mahogany, and lots of others. We began making the trays. They came out real nice. We put glass in them.

Each tray would hold seven or eight butterflies. I put the biggest one in the center and worked the others around it. I got some white cotton over at the storehouse and put this in the trays first.

Then I placed the butterflies on it next to the glass. They sure looked nice.

After we got finished, I made up several trays. I had one tray of Blue Emperors, which were very rare. There were hundreds of varieties over there. Well we got some made up. I think the guys decided we hadn't lost our marbles, just part of them.

My, this did help relieve the stress. We had fun while we were doing it. Just about the time we got the butterflies fixed up, we got word we would be held hostage again. All the other companies would move out. We would have to clean up the whole island, anything that the U.S. had left. What a huge job that was going to be!

The first thing we did was to get the old D8 twin stacks high output dozers and started pushing big long trenches. They would have to be ten or twelve feet deep and enough to make three or four miles long. There was everything imaginable here. We would have to put the big stuff in first, then the next biggest and so on until we would get it all in the big trench. This would take several weeks.

There were lots of big 6 x 6 trucks, jeeps, boom trucks, backhoes, fire trucks, and all kinds of tools. There were hand tools, mechanic tools, carpenter tools, chain saws, big water pumps, big gasoline tanks and diesel tanks. Then there were tents, hundreds of them, officer's barracks, and medical supplies. You name it we had to bury it.

The last thing that went in was the old D8 dozers. Then we covered them by hand. Now everything was taken care of but the chemical ammo dump. We were given orders to load it up and take it to the barge where it would be hauled out into the Pacific Ocean about seven or eight miles and dumped into the ocean. This would take several weeks or months. There were several hundred tons to get rid of.

We finally got the job done. Then we were told we would have to wait for a troop ship to come and get us. War had been over about six months. We were still held hostage on the island. It looked like we might be here four or five more weeks before the ship would come in. There was nothing to do now, not even anything to eat.

We would be living like the natives, eating coconuts and drinking the milk. We got a few bananas now and then and there was a little other fruit that grew here. There was still a little bit of stuff left in the garden we could eat until it was gone. Drinking water was a problem. There was no way to purify it.

Three weeks had passed since we cleaned up the chemical dump. We had heard rumors that a ship might come in the next week. I was sure hoping so. It was hard to wait in a situation like this. The stress factor just kept building up. We thought we would not have enough time to catch more butterflies and take care of them. So we just walked around waiting and hoping.

Sure enough the ship finally got there. It would take two or three days to get loaded up and get rid of our tents and some other little things we had been using. There was hardly anything sent back to the U.S. The government made a deal with manufacturers that they wouldn't bring any of the stuff back to the U.S.A. and hurt their market on jeeps and things like that.

We were all finally on the ship. We would pull out for the good old U.S.A. in the morning. It would stop at some of the other islands and load and unload some people and things. We knew it would take a few weeks to get back.

> We were all finally on the ship. We would pull out for the good old U.S.A. in the morning

The second day out we had a little problem. We ran into a typhoon and steered around it for one day so it wouldn't be too bad. We stopped at several pretty islands as we came back. The first one was Samoa Island. We pulled in dock there. The native men were sure friendly. We would throw coins in the deep water and the natives would dive down in the deep water and bring the coins up. They made quite a bit of money diving down in the water and getting the coins. They called everybody "Joe". I guess that was short for GI Joe. We got to get on the island. They had little huts with dirt floors. They were pretty good compared to what we had been living in.

There wasn't any work to do on the island, so they danced, fished, and swam for entertainment and to put in their time.

They danced and entertained us for a little while. We got to get back on the boat by night. We would pull out in the morning. After all this entertainment, we were in pretty good shape. We were ready to load out for the U.S.A.

After two or three days of the same old thing, all you could see was water, sea gulls, and big fish jumping. This was all we had to do, wait and watch. Sometimes you would get some KP duty, guard duty, or clean up duty. I didn't mind that. It helped to pass the time by. We had been on the water several days.

We made another stop at one of the islands. By morning we were back on the ship heading out. It wouldn't be too long before we would get to Hawaii. We had been on the ship several days again. We could begin to see land. The closer we got the more you could see. Sure enough we were docked there one night and one day. My, there was a lot to see there. They really entertained the soldiers that were coming home from war.

Our time was all gone and we would be getting on the ship that night. We had pulled out about daylight. This would be the home stretch on water. It would take a day or two to get back to the U.S.A. We were just out in the big ocean. All you could see was lots of water, whales, big fish, and some birds, mostly sea gulls. They followed the ship to get the waste food from the kitchen of the ship.

Day two at 8 PM it looked like we could see land a ways off. Hopefully this would be it. By noon it was looking better all the time. We could see the golden-gate bridge. My, did that ever look good. We went right under it and in a little while we were docked at the state of California. Well, after a few hours they had a convoy of army trucks there to take us to the army base.

They let us off at the kitchen. They had a big meal of turkey, dressing, ham, mashed potatoes, gravy, coffee, and all the milk you could drink prepared for us. We almost foundered. It was quite a deal after eating out of cans, sea rations, and off the island for three years.

Anyway I was disappointed when we got off the ship at California. There wasn't anyone there to meet us. There was no music or anything. It seemed like the workers around there wondered why they brought us back to the U.S.A.

We would have to hang around here for two or three days. Then they would put us on different trains to send us home. We would all be going to different states. There were several of us going to Kansas.

Sure enough they started sending us out to different places. Some would be going south, some out east, and just about all over the U.S.A. Anyone from Missouri or Kansas got on the same train.

We loaded up one morning and headed to Leavenworth, Kansas. That was where we would be released. We would be held here for a few days. They would give us a physical. We knew what the outcome would be before we got it. They didn't find anything wrong with anybody. Some could hardly walk. Some were shot up, but everyone got a good clean bill of health put on their record.

After we got a good clean health record, they put me on a bus that was going to Missouri. Then when it got to Kansas City, I had to change buses. I got another bus out of Kansas City that was going south to Springfield.

After about two hours ride, we got to Fristoe, Missouri where they let me off to go home. This was about one o'clock at night. It was about ten miles out to the farm where my home was. There were no telephones. It was in the part of the county that there was no electricity and not very many cars. People were poor and hard up. They couldn't afford one. Well, anyway I had a choice. I could lay down there on the ground and wait for daylight or I could start walking home. There were a few stars out. You could see a little. So I decided to walk.

I had a duffle bag full of clothes and other things. It was pretty heavy. I didn't have any flashlight, but I knew the road real well. It was just an old wagon road that farmers used to go get groceries now and then. Well, I was doing pretty well. I had been walking two hours or so. I wasn't making very good time. I was carrying a pretty heavy load, but I was getting closer home.

I got down to the old Bybee place. They had changed the road. There was a creek to cross. I couldn't see very well, only a few feet. The creek had been up pretty high, but had run down to about normal. The thing I didn't know was the water had washed out the barbed wire fence and it was stretched out over the road in the water. I didn't want to wade it and get wet, so I threw my luggage across the creek. Then I backed up, took a big run, and jumped the water. It worked except for the fact that I caught my toe on the barbed wire fence. I fell when I got to the other side. One hand fell on a sharp flat rock. It bled quite a bit.

There wasn't much need to pay any attention to that. It was more important to try to get home. I picked up my luggage and started up the hill on a new road that I had never run in the dark. Finally I got to the top of the hill. Then I was back on the old road. I could tell where I was then.

It would be daylight in about one hour, but I would be home in about thirty minutes or less. The folks didn't know that I was coming home that night. They were just getting up when I knocked on the door. My, were we ever glad to see one another. I still had one brother and one sister at home. My, we had a good time talking and catching up on all the news.

Mom started breakfast. She could tell I was worn out and tired. Anyway she cooked me up a big breakfast. I had about three eggs, several pieces of bacon, and we always had homemade biscuits for breakfast and red-eyed gravy. There was always the molasses pitcher on the table, our own cow butter, and mom always had some kind of jelly all the time.

Well anyway, I got good and full. I was sitting in the old chair and fell off to sleep. So mom fixed the bed and said go get a little rest. I did. I didn't sleep too long till I was wide awake.

I wanted to look around at the old farm. Most everything looked the same. There had been a few changes. Dad had raised up some different cows and he had one new horse. He had made a few changes in some of the fences. I helped dad around the farm for a few weeks. I was still in shock. I couldn't believe I was home. I had what they now call post trauma stress disorder real bad and would have it the rest of my life.

I thought I had better get out and get me a car. I found one at Cross Timbers, a real sharp looking Plymouth. So I bought it. I drove it for a little while, but the motor was bad. I couldn't keep the rod from blowing in it. So I started working around at different farm jobs. That gave me money to fix my car with. The motor got so bad, I finally got rid of it.

I found an old 29 Model A car. It had a rumble seat and cloth top that would lay down. This was really a good old car. A banker had bought it new and took real good care of it. Even the girls all wanted a ride in this old Model A. The first Christmas I had the old car I decorated it up and put a Christmas tree in the rumble seat. It looked pretty good. I went to Climax Springs, Missouri and drove around a little. I think everybody liked my Christmas tree.

I was still having trouble with the post trauma stress disorder pretty bad, but doctors didn't know what that was or how to doctor me. This was something I was going to have to live with the rest of my life. I had been home several months now. I had a breakdown ever so often. But I seemed to get better in a few days.

I had returned to Benton County, Missouri in April of 1946. By this time I had been home several months.

# 1947

It was spring of 1947. I thought maybe I would start dating, by this time. I went to old Climax Springs about every Saturday. I just happened to be in the right place at the right time. I was coming down the old school house road and there was a 1937 Chevy, real nice looking car, pulled out in front of me. In the back seat there was a nice looking young girl. So I followed the car on through town and up the hill. This little girl just kept looking back at me and smiling.

In a few days or by the next Saturday I found out where she lived. I got up the nerve to drive down there to her house. Well, I got there. My, what I didn't know was that her dad was a foxhunter and he had a lot of hounds. They all came running out and barking at me. I didn't know whether they were glad to see me or wanted to bite me.

After they calmed down a little, I decided to get out. I almost got cold feet before I got to the door. Anyway, I finally got there, knocked on the door, and Mr. Keltner came to the door. He asked if he could help me.

I stuttered around a little and finally got it out. I said, "Is your daughter Claudine here."

He said, "I think so."

I could tell by the tone of his voice he wasn't quite ready for her to start dating. I understand that now, but I didn't then.

She asked him if she could go out with me.

He said, "No, maybe later."

I left, but in a couple of weeks I was back. I went down there again. The dogs greeted me a little better this time. So I got my nerve up and went to the door again. Mrs. Keltner came to the door this time. She invited me in. Claudine and I talked a little while. I just asked her mom if Claudine could go with me to old Climax Springs, Missouri. I promised her I would have her home by four o'clock in the evening. Her mom said yes she could go.

We went back to town. There wasn't much to do, but lots of other couples were around there to visit with. There was a big spring at the edge of town. Seemed like a lot of young people hung out there.

This old spring was a real old landmark for the town of Climax Springs, Missouri. There was a big two-story hotel down by the spring. Back in horse and buggy day people would come to town and stay all night at the old hotel. There were barns and stalls for the horses and they watered them out of the spring. This was quite a place. In fact, it was the only place around that you could rent a bed, have a place for your team, and get feed for them and people could also eat there.

There were several grocery stores and a feed store, a filling station, a big bank, and a small theater. There were a couple of garages, a grade school and high school, post office, and a big stone mill up on the hill above the old spring. The old spring is still running today and the old hotel is still standing. Someone lives in it yet. There were three or four churches going strong by this time.

My, Saturday was a big day for Climax Springs. There were lots of teams and wagons, horse backers, and there was getting to be a lot of cars and trucks in town also. There was a big hill on the east side of town. It wasn't unusual to see twenty-five or thirty cars parked on the hill. Most everyone was young people, just talking and having a good time. There were still several young guys coming to town on horseback if they didn't have a car.

By this time Claudine and I had been dating several months. We decided to get married. Back then most everyone was married by the justice of the peace. Since Claudine was a Christian, she wanted a preacher to marry us. She knew someone who had been the pastor of her church.

We got our better clothes on. I had about one hundred dollars in my pocket. We headed out to Camdenton, Missouri and told the pastor what we wanted. He talked to us a little while. He knew Claudine was a Christian.
He asked me if I had been saved. Well, I had to say no.

He stopped right there and said young man. I don't marry people if they are not both Christians.

By this time I was feeling bad. He talked to us a while and finally said. Well, I guess I'll marry you anyway.

So he called his wife in as a witness. He went on with the ceremony. Boy, was I ever getting hot. I had a necktie on. I was about to choke to death.

Finally it was over. I thanked him and paid him. We had enough money left to get a motel room and the evening meal. We stayed all night, got up the next day and drove around Camdenton. We looked at some of the main attractions there. Then we went to Ha Ha Tonka and looked around there awhile.

We came home and told my folks what had happened. They greeted us and invited us in. We talked a while and then said we were going to old knobby to try to rent or buy a house since

Claudine had a contract with the Ritter School District to teach school that year. She would teach all eight grades.

We found this older type house. It set up on a big hill. It was a real nice house. We got it rented for that year. Back then there wasn't any insulation put in houses. They didn't even make any at that time. Well, anyway, this was the fall of the year. By this time we had to think about getting a wood-heating stove. We already had a wood cook stove, one bed, a table and four chairs. We were just kind of getting started out in our new married life.

Winter was about here. We had to get out and cut some wood. There were no chain saws, just a good sharp chopping axe. I had chopped for several days. I didn't have a team or wagon then. I had got one horse and broke her to ride. I needed to break her to work. I harnessed her up and drove her single for a few days.

It was time to drag some logs to the house. I had cut the trees down and trimmed them up good, all the way to the top. They were five or six inches at the bottom and twenty-five or thirty feet long. I hitched on for the first time. I said, "Get up," and away we went. Everything was okay until she looked back and saw this long pole flopping around. She started trying to run off. I managed to keep up till we got to the big hill. The log was heavy and the hill was steep and long. She was still scared and trying to run away. I kept hanging on. By the time we got over the big hill she was worn down some, so we made it on up to the woodpile.

I unhooked and went back and hooked on another long pole. She did better this time. We dragged poles all day. By night she was working like a well broke horse. I unhitched her and put her in the barn that evening. I had lots of good hay and some grain for her. She was a black mare with a white star and four white socks, pretty big and real fat. She was three years old when I started with her.

It looked like the weather would be bad in a few days. I chopped those long poles up into 18 inch pieces so they would fit in the old heating stove. I chopped for several days and ran out of long poles. It was time to drag some more in.

Well I got Black Beauty harnessed up and we headed for the timber. I hooked onto a pretty big pole, and said, get up to Beauty. Away we went heading for the big hill. She was a little excited, but not too bad. Over the hill we went. By this time Beauty was acting like a well broke horse. I worked all day dragging logs. I had a pretty good pile by nightfall.

Claudine was teaching at the old Ritter School every day. On real bad days I would take her to school and then chop wood the rest of the day.

By this time I had a lot of good wood cut up and piled. The old house was sure hard to heat. It was made out of oak 2 X 4 studs with ½ X 6 inch siding on the outside. It looked good, but no insulation in the walls, just plaster on the inside, and some paper on the inside too. It had a 1 X 6 oak floor. Oak would shrink so there would be big cracks in the floor. We got a 9 X 12 foot linoleum rug and put over part of it. It sure looked good compared to the oak boards.

The house was facing the southeast, sitting on a hill. There wasn't any concrete foundation, so it was sitting on rocks stacked up at the corners and in the middle of the house. Also the backside of the house was close to the ground.

When it was cold and windy, the wind blew under the old house real bad. We put the table and four chairs in the middle of the new 9 X 12 rug and when the wind would blow real hard the table and chairs would just jump up and down. We had the heating stove in this room also. When the wind blew real hard I would take some of the big sticks and put around the edge of the new rug. This would help hold it down.

We always had a bucket of fresh water out of the well and set it by the old wood-heating stove. Sometimes the dipper would freeze to the bucket, so we would put it on top of the stove and thaw it out.

# 1948

The cold weather went on for several months. It was a pretty hard winter. Spring finally came. We didn't have to cut much wood, only for the cook stove. That took quite a bit of time. The wood had to be cut shorter and split real fine. It also had to be real dry. This would make a good hot fire.

Claudine would cook breakfast every morning. My, she was a fine biscuit maker, as well as a real cook. For breakfast we always had good white gravy or red-eyed gravy and butter to go with them. Sometimes we had bacon or ham when we could afford it. Almost everybody had homemade sorghum so there was molasses on the table for every meal. It was very healthy. Back then we ate a lot of pork and a lot of grease. When we fried ham we made red-eyed gravy out of the grease. You just added a little water and about four tablespoons of coffee. Stir this all up and cook it. My, this and hot biscuits were sure good. We used hog lard all the time and lots of it. The Food and Health Administration has put out information about pork and grease for several years telling us how bad it is for our health. Well, that didn't seem to always be so. All the farm families and all my folks had used pork and grease all their lives. There were two things that needed to be done. Keep the molasses pitcher on the table three times a day and work hard. Dad's parents lived to be almost one hundred years old and ninety percent of all the old farmers that I knew lived to be an old, old age.

Back then there wasn't any refrigeration, so pork was about all the meat you could keep the year around. The old timers salted and sugar cured all their pork and kept it year around. Salt and sugar are supposed to be bad for our health, but it didn't seem to hurt the old timers.

> Salt and sugar are supposed to be bad for our health, but it didn't seem to hurt the old timers.

They lived on pork, grease, sugar, and salt. They lived to be an old age, and most never went to a doctor. There weren't many doctors back then. Just keep that molasses pitcher on the table and work hard. You might live to be one hundred years old too.

Well, it was up in the summer by now. Claudine's school was out so she was home making garden. I was still working out for different farmers. Times were still pretty hard, but seemed to be getting better. There was a little more work now. This part of Missouri was getting a little more modern than it had been.

There was getting to be several tractors in the county now. The 8N Ford was real popular. Also the International Harvester Tractor A, C, H, and M were all getting popular. Machinery was getting a lot more modern and better than it was. There were balers, mowers, rakes, and everything else. This sure helped in getting the farming and haying done.

The very first baler was horse drawn and powered by horses. By now they had a few out that had a motor mounted on them to power the baler. My, this sure took a load off of the old horses.

Everything was square baled up till this time. Alice Chalmers had come out with a small round baler, first of its kind. This little baler made fifty to seventy pound round bales. You could leave the bales lying in the field and just turn the cattle in on them when winter came. This saved a lot of work feeding everyday.

Things were just getting quite a bit better on the farm. By this time we had moved over to the rock house by the old Antioch School House. We hadn't been married very long. We didn't have any money, or much furniture.

We went to a big furniture store in Buffalo, Missouri. We picked out a nice chrome breakfast table, red and white, with four chairs. Then we picked out a three-piece bedroom set. It included the bed, mattress, chest of drawers, and dresser with mirror. Since I was working on the farm and Claudine was teaching school we didn't have a lot of money. The furniture owner said he would charge it since we were just getting started with a new married life.

He said, "Now for your wedding present I will give you a full set of dishes and a full set of silverware. He also threw in lots of other little things that we needed. My, what a nice man he was. We thanked him from the bottom of our hearts. What a great guy he was!

Claudine was so proud of her new furniture. She said I believe that is the prettiest table I have ever seen. Well anyway we got started with that. We still needed lots of other little things like brooms, mops, bedding, towels, and tea towels. We needed wash clothes, cleaning supplies, soaps and the list goes on. We continued to gradually get the other things we needed. But we never forgot what a blessing the furniture was. Thanks again to the furniture store man.

# 1949

We had been there for several months and we wanted to buy a farm. Early one morning my uncle Henry and Aunt Velma Berryman came over and said they wanted to sell their family farm. We went over and looked at the farm. We really liked it. It sure was a nice place, about two hundred acres, some good farmland, and some good timberland. We said we would see if we could come up with the money. They wanted three thousand dollars for the farm. I had just got out of the army a little over two years before so I hadn't done any banking anywhere, only a little at the Citizen's Bank. This was a pretty big deal back then. It wouldn't be much now fifty some years later.

I decided to go to the Community Bank of Warsaw. My what a nice banker he was. I told him I was a veteran, just back from World War II and that I would like to get a farm of my own, but didn't have any money.

He said, "Do you have any place in mind."

I said, "Yes, the Berryman place is for sale for three thousand dollars."

He answered, "Young man, I don't know you, but we try to help all the men that went to serve and to protect our country." So he said he would come out to look at the farm.

When he came, I told him what I had in mind to do. After we got back to the house he said, "I don't know you, but I like what I see." He was a great man in the bank and to the community. After we got through talking he told me to come in to the bank in the morning and we would fix up a loan. The people at this bank were some of the best friends I had.

We had a few good years so I got the farm paid off pretty early. Anyway, after we bought the farm, I began to put some crops out. I had already bought another mare to match Black Beauty. I had to break her out while I was trying to get the crops out. I didn't have any cattle yet.

I had a 1947 Mercury, so I thought I would trade it for cattle. I found a bunch of milking shorthorn heifers for sale this side of Warsaw. A mighty nice old gentleman owned them. He wanted a little newer car. He had a 1935 Chrysler. This was the biggest car they made in 1935. It had a straight eight motor in it. It had a spare tire built in each front fender with chrome bands around them. My, this was a nice old car. I went and looked at the heifers. He had thirty some of them to pick from.

He said, "Young man, you can pick five of the heifers and I'll trade them and my 1935 Chrysler for your 1947 Mercury."

Well, that was a good deal for both of us. I picked five of the biggest that would calve in a few months. I got them home. It wasn't long till I had five calves on the ground. They all turned out to be good milk cows, as well as good calf raisers.

It was time to start milking. Back then you could sell grade C milk. There was a grade C truck that ran every day in this part of the country. I broke all five of the heifers to milk. I had to milk by hand. Back then there was no electricity. I bought me some ten gallon cream cans. I started out with one can. Finally, I got to where I needed another can. My, this was really helping. The milkman brought me a check every two weeks. I kept all the heifer calves and sold the bull calves when they got to be four hundred pounds or so.

There were always several revivals going on. We went to the old Wiseman School House during one of their revivals for a little entertainment. The man who was preaching was a circuit rider preacher and had been most of his life. But now he had a car. We got to the old school house and he welcomed us and invited us in.

He said, "We have two seats on the front row just for you."

Did he ever preach hard. I got hot. Then I got air born and landed up front before I knew what had happened. I was still getting hotter and hotter. I think everyone in the house was praying for me. My, what a relief it was when I accepted Christ as my Savior.

> I think everyone in the house was praying for me. My, what a relief it was when I accepted Christ as my Savior.

I started out after church was over and people said, "Glen I thought you were a Christian."

I was living the good life, but I didn't have God fooled and I knew I wasn't saved too.

In 1949 R.E.A. was putting in an electric line down past the farm. I began to wire up the old log house. I got me a book from R.E.A. to see what the rules were. Later in the fall they came by to hook me up. They inspected my wiring job and said the home wiring was fine, but the entrance cable was too long. He said if I would get up there and shorten the cable a little they would turn on the electricity. So I did. He said we were the first to get hooked up on the new line. All the others had something wrong. The others all had electricians do their work, but they were not familiar with R.E.A. regulations.

I didn't know much about electricity at this time. I just went by the book. We hooked up to the electric line, but all we had was lights. We didn't have any appliances at all. Times were still rough. We were trying to put our extra money to pay off farm expenses. Well, anyway we finally got a new refrigerator. It cost sixty-nine dollars and ninety-five cents. That was a lot of money back then. Now we could keep our milk more than one day. Besides that, it was good and cold to drink. It had a big freezer compartment in it, so we could even have a place to put meat and other things. It sure was nice.

As the years went on we finally got a toaster, mixer, and several other things. I needed a truck to use on the farm, so I traded my 1935 Chrysler for a 1941 half-ton Ford pick-up. It sure helped to have a truck. I could haul a calf or two off to the market and a lot of other uses on the farm as well.

We were still working hard. I had lots of health problems from being in World War II. Training in the chemical testing fields and having served in the Chemical Warfare Company during my army life had taken its toll. I had developed Post Trauma Stress while in the army. No one then knew much about it or how to doctor you. The live mustard agent moves around very slowly in your system, attacking different organs as it travels around. I had to work at trying to keep my body strong.

# 1950

Winter is over. It is springtime in the Ozarks. I had the garden plowed. Some things were ready to plant, and guess what else was happening. We were getting good spring rains. Everything looked so good. They were giving storm warnings on the radio, no TV yet. It was just a little after dark. We had the door open. It was nice and warm. All at once, we heard this loud roaring and the wind got real high. My, by this time it was really looking bad. As it was lightning you could see the outside toilet floating through the sky. Pieces of metal off the old barn and hen house were flying. I yelled, "Shut the front door." Then we ran to the back door. By this time there was a vacuum and it jerked the door out of my hand and slammed it shut real hard. When it did we couldn't get the door open to go to the cellar. Finally the tornado passed. I still couldn't get the door open.

> By this time there was a vacuum and it jerked the door out of my hand and slammed it shut real hard.

The next day I took the old lock apart and fixed it. The tornado had torn up a lot of things around the farm. A big maple tree fell on part of the old log house. It had windows broke out.

It was daylight by now, so I could see what was wrong outside. I went to milk and turn the calf in to suck. The calf was gone and I couldn't find it. I got my horse up and started riding the field and woodland. About noon, I found him. He had been picked up by the tornado and carried through the brush for one-fourth mile. He was burnt on the back where he lost his hair going through the trees in the air. I got him back to the house to his mother.

My folks lived on the old homestead about one and one half miles away. They had chopped their way over to our place. The roads were all full of trees lying across them. They said it blew the top of the house off and blew the barn down, but the milk cows were still in it. Some were dead. Some were bawling and mooing in pain. I got my ax and went back over with them. We began chopping the big timber up. Finally we got one out. She jumped up and ran to the other side of the farm. Then we started on another one that was bawling. Finally we got her out. We cut out about four or five cows that were still alive, but there were still several dead ones under the boards. Some even had 2 X 4s run through them. Some had broken necks and many other injuries.

Old Pearl was the favorite milk cow. She was in bad shape when we got her out from under the barn. She couldn't walk, so we carried her feed and water for several months. She finally died. This was a big loss for dad. He lost several cows, a barn, and most of the house.

When things began to settle a little, we bought lumber and started to rebuild the old house. We put up all new rafters, sheeting, and shingles. Several neighbors came in and helped us. We had the house back in order in a few days.

Now the next thing was the barn. We cut logs and took them to the sawmill and got enough lumber sawed out to build the barn back. Some of the old barn lumber was still good. We used some of the new and the old. My Uncle Loren Welch was a good carpenter so he came over and stayed to help put the barn back together. Things had finally begun to let up a little around here so I was spending most of my time back home catching up.

The garden was pretty good this year. Claudine had done a lot of canning. It was going to be hay time before long. I had been working on the old horse mower and got the sickle sharpened and the machine greased up. I had put a new tongue in it last year. I just needed to make one new single tree and then I would be ready to go.

I guess the next thing was to shoe the team with new metal horseshoes. I was going to oil the harness before I started haying. This would sure help the harness last longer. This was always quite a little chore.

I would put several gallons of harness oil in a barrel and then I would put water on the harness before putting it in the oil.

I would take three poles and make a tripod over the barrel and hang the harness up to drip back in the barrel. When they were completely dry, I would take them down and they were ready to use again. My harness never rotted out. They just wore out. Fifty years later I am still using and oiling my harness just like I did back then. Anyway I was going to start cutting hay the next day. It would take a long time to put the hay up. You could only cut two or three acres with a five-foot horse mower in one day. I had to work on the old horse dump rake. I had to take the wheels off and pack them and do other little repairs. There was a fence to fix where the trees had blown down across it. The next day I would start raking with the old dump rake. They were what you called dump rakes because they had a foot dump on them. You just started driving around the field. You had to dump it about every two hundred feet, depending on how good the hay was. This would make a windrow of hay. This would take all day to rake what I had cut two days before.

The next day we would start stacking the hay for the new rick. We had an old bull rake about twelve feet wide. You put a horse on each side of it. This rake had wooden teeth about eight feet long and about twelve inches apart. This would bring in a lot of hay at one time. You just drove down the windrow till the rake got full. Then pull out and go to where they were going to make a haystack.

It took two guys with pitchforks to pitch the hay up on the stack. One man would place the hay around and make a nice round haystack. The other would walk it down good. One of the neighbors would always say, "Just walk like you are going to Climax Springs to the store." It took a lot of walking to make a good solid stack that would turn the water and keep till spring.

That was the way we hayed and it would go on all summer even up in the fall. I always got up an hour or so before daylight, lit the lantern, went to the barn, fed the horses, started the milking, and always tried to get in two hours of work before breakfast.

After breakfast I would go carry the old team's harness and take it out to the watering tank. By this time it was getting daylight and I was in the field. You could see pretty well by now. I was still having trouble with the Post Trauma Stress. The only way to control it was to work real hard. This helped to keep my body strong and I would be tired enough at night to sleep better.

Finally I got the hay all put up as well as the other crops too. The next thing was to fence the haystacks. Then I could go out in the winter and take my pitchfork and feed off of the haystack. This always worked pretty well.

It had been a good open winter to feed. Our oldest daughter Pauletta came along. My, what a blessing this was. We always went to church every Sunday and after Pauletta was a couple of weeks old, Claudine made her some new little clothes and even a little red cap with lace on it. My, we were proud parents. This was the first one, so of course we took her to church for everyone to see.

# 1951

It was 1951 and we were getting a lot of rains. The weatherman said this might go on for some time. Sure enough when the old earth got soaked up we began to have floods. All the branches were really big and the big river was flooding. Kansas City was hit pretty hard. High water got up in the Kansas City stockyards. It washed all the animals down the river. You could see hogs and cattle floating everywhere. Some would hang on buildings or housetops.

Anything close to the Missouri River or the Kaw River that came out of Kansas was ruined. It just ruined several thousand homes and businesses all up and down the two rivers. There were lots of other people's homes destroyed by smaller creeks and branches.

> Anything close to the Missouri River or the Kaw River that came out of Kansas was ruined.

It tore up roads and bridges. Water lines, sewer lines, wells, and electric lines were all destroyed. Piled sand and debris were all over people's property.

My, the clean up cost people, insurance companies, and the government millions of dollars. Lots of people and companies never did get over this. It was a big disaster for Missouri and the joining states. It took months and even years to get things partly cleaned up.

There were a lot of big ads in the papers for needed help. So I decided to go to the city and work for a while. Hobson Caterpillar Company had a big ad in the Kansas City paper needing help to clean up. Their company; all the parts, most of their buildings, tractors, trucks, and almost everything had been under water.

I went to Kansas City to Hobson and Company and put in my application.

They hired me right then and said, "Can you start now." So I did. I worked the rest of the week. I always came back down to the farm every weekend. I told several of my friends about Hobson and Company and that I could get them a job. Several from Benton County, Missouri came up and got right on. Two of these guys I helped get a job stayed with Hobson until retirement age.

# 1952-1953

The year was 1952. By this time our second daughter had come along. What a blessing this was. We were really proud of her. Pauletta was two years old and she wasn't sure about this deal since she didn't get all the attention any more. Finally she decided her sister Janet could be her doll. That worked out pretty good.

The girls grew up together and were real close. Whatever one did the other one would do too. When Janet was about two weeks old, Claudine was feeling better. She had made her some new little pink clothes. We could take her to church and show everyone. The girls brought great joy to our family.

I was still working in Kansas City for Hobson and Company. I had been there about three years. I was thinking about moving back to the farm. I had been keeping my heifers for three years now so I had gotten my cowherd built up pretty good.

# 1954

It was the spring of 1954. There was plenty of rain. Everything looked pretty good. I was putting in some crops between showers. The cows were beginning to have their spring calves again this year. This would make me about fifty head of cows. There were several cattle buyers coming around. Things were looking good. Some of the buyers offered me pretty big money, fifty five hundred for about thirty cows and several calves. I turned it down. I thought they would be worth a lot more by fall. What I didn't know was the rains would quit about the first of June. The cows had finished calving and the rains completely stopped. Not even a shower. Grass was getting shorter. Ponds were going dry. Back then the ponds weren't very good or very big. Most of them had been built with teams, plows, and slips. You loaded by hand. It took several months to build even a small pond with a couple of teams.

Well, it was coming on fall of 1954. It was real hot and dry and had been for five months now. The grass was all burnt up. The ponds were all dried up. There weren't any drilled wells that were good. Back then most of them were twenty to sixty foot deep. Everyone was selling their cattle off and had been for a couple of months. The market was loaded. The price was down to nothing. I was going to have to sell. I had no grass or water. So I contacted some of the buyers that had been there in the spring. They told me the same thing. The market is down to nothing and the stockyards were full. It seemed that the rains for this year was over.

One of them said, "I'll come and look at your cows." This was the same guy who had offered me fifty-five hundred dollars in the spring. I should have taken his offer then. Well, he looked at the cattle. I had ten more calves now than when he looked at them in the spring. We walked around the herd.

They looked good. He said, "This isn't much, but I'll give one thousand three hundred dollars for all sixty head."

I didn't have any choice. They were out of water and no way to water them. I said, "Well, I guess I'll have to sell them to you since I don't have any water or grass."

This was a big loss. I lost four thousand two hundred dollars in one summer plus all my work and other expenses. We were sure sick around here for several months. No cattle and not much money. I got out and started doing construction work. I built houses, barns, those big chicken houses, and whatever there was to do.

> I lost four thousand two hundred dollars in one summer plus all my work and other expenses.

# 1955-1956

The drought broke in 1955. I began to pick me up a few cows now and then. I got started back. Our first little boy was born. We named him David. Was I ever proud of him. Claudine had two little girls and now I had a boy. We were so proud of him. Of course we had to fix him up and take him to church. You know it is always good to get to show off your kids. Well, anyway, we were sure proud of all our kids. The girls were growing and getting bigger. They thought it was okay to have a baby brother to take care of. In fact they would pretend they were the mommy taking care of the baby. That all worked out good too. It sure helped Claudine get the housework done while the girls were taking care of David. We had begun to get a little more rain. It looked like we might have a little bit of hay to put up. It wouldn't be any good, but it would beat a snow bank.

In 1956 the U.S. Army was going to build a lot of Barracks in Knobnoster, Missouri and other buildings too. I went up and got a job. Pay was good back then, but it was a long way to drive to work every day. There were several guys working up there from Edwards and Cross Timbers, so we were driving to Whiteman Air Force Base at Knobnoster, Missouri. Transportation was a problem. Little Joe out at Cross Timbers said he was going to buy a new 1956 Ford top of the line car. He was proud of that car and we were too. He would drive everyday and take us to work. We would pay him so much a day to ride with him. This sure helped us and helped him too. So thanks to Little Joe. We sure did appreciate it. That job lasted a couple of years. Then I went back to the farm full time. I was going to do more farming this time, put out several acres of oats and a little corn. I always liked to have oat hay to feed to the milk cows. My, it would sure make the milk taste better and they would give more milk. It was good for the workhorses too.

We were still going to church regular. Every time the church doors were open we were there helping. The Old Baptist Church was set in downtown Climax Springs on a hill on the northeast side of town. The old church had been there almost a hundred years. It was getting in bad shape. By this time the state had put in a new road about one fourth mile from the old church. Later the road would become a blacktop highway. The church wanted to buy two acres of highway frontage to build a new church on in the near future.

> Every time the church doors were open we were there helping.

# 1957-1958

The year 1957 was a pretty good year with plenty of rain. Crops were good and it was a good year for us because our last baby boy was born. Claudine named him Mark Alan. She picked out Bible names for the boys. My, were we ever proud of Mark. He was to be the last one. The girls had another baby brother to take care of while Claudine was doing the housework. They always wanted to feed him and hold the baby bottle.

Anyway by this time he was a few days old. Claudine had new clothes made up for him. We could take him to church and show him off. We always thought we had four of the best kids there ever was anywhere. We never had a baby sitter. We always took the kids wherever we went. We went to church every time the church door was open. We all sat in the same pew with the four kids in the middle. Their mother was a good disciplinarian. She always disciplined them in love. I helped a little.

We have been to several big farm meetings and church meetings. Sometimes there would be a big meal involved and these four little kids would sit right at the table just like the grown-ups. You never heard a word out of them. You would have thought they were all adults. They weren't only good kids then, they are still the best I know of.

We always have been a real close family. Claudine and I were both saved before we started our family. God's love has always been with us. This made it so much easier to raise a family. To this day, all our children and most of the grandkids are saved. We keep Christ in the center. At Christmas time we always read the Christmas story in Luke. We always keep Christ in the center of the Christmas season. Families that pray together, stay together.

> We always keep Christ in the center of the Christmas season. Families that pray together, stay together.

In 1957, I got a chance to work for a John Deere dealership in Kansas City, Missouri. My, this was a good job. I became the demonstrator for the John Deere tractor and all the machinery. I had a real good salesman that I worked with. Most of the big farmers had I.H.C. tractors and machinery at this time. So the salesman's job was to convince the farmers that he had a much better product then the one they were using. John Deere had come out with bigger and better tractors and machinery at this time. The salesman did a real good job of selling the John Deere equipment. About every day, I would drive a new John Deere tractor across Kansas City and over to the river bottom farms. Then I would drive the old tractor back across Kansas City. It wasn't only tractors. Sometimes it was those big sixteen-foot combines.

Back then it wasn't too bad. Most people drove slower and had respect for the other people on the road. Now it would be almost impossible to drive a sixteen-foot combine across Sixth Street Bridge to get back to Kansas City. Times have really changed and people have changed too. I think the John Deere salesman changed almost every farmer over to a John Deere tractor and equipment.

We had lots of plowing demonstrations in the river bottoms. They had to plow in old black gumbo that pulled really hard. By this time John Deere had went from the old 70 John Deere to the 720 John Deere tractor, both in gas and diesel. This was a big improvement and lots more power. John Deere was pretty much leading the race by this time. They had more horsepower. Every time we had a plowing contest, we would win because of the extra horsepower.

At that time we were pulling four sixteen inch plows and did it ever pull hard in that black gumbo soil. The black smoke would just roll from those diesel tractors. It was always a fun day to plow and win. As the years went by Kansas City just kept getting bigger, crowded, and lots more traffic. It just squeezed the John Deere dealership out. It had to move. So at that time I came back to the farm.

# 1959-1961

By this time the kids were getting older and bigger. The city wasn't a very good place to raise a family. We came back to the farm and I was working full time in the church. Claudine and I helped with the youth. We would go early, go down in old Climax Springs and gather up kids of all ages. We went out in the country and gathered up too. We always had snacks for them. We used to let them eat first and then do a lesson. Some of the oldest kids just came and ate and then left. We decided to change our plan. We would have the lesson first and tell them about Jesus. Then we would eat. This worked out a lot better.

We always tried to do something for the youth. We would take them skating once or twice a month, have a ball game, baseball, softball, volleyball, anything to keep them coming back. We could tell them about Christ and how he would save them. We worked at this for twenty years or so until all of our children were grown and on their own.

We always did community work. We kept the kids in 4H. The boys had horses to use in the 4H and the saddle club. They both won a lot of trophies for barrel racing, pole bending, the pick up race, and the egg and spoon race. They both got pretty good. The competition was getting greater all the time. The youngest boy won in the county competition, so he got to go all the way to state. It seemed like I hauled those boys and their horses a million miles, but I guess it wasn't near that far. Anyway I worked hard to keep them interested in horses and keep them out of fast cars as long as I could.

We had been back on the farm for some time now. I got a chance to raise turkeys for a big feed company. My brother-in-law had been raising chickens and now he was raising turkeys. At that time you didn't have to have a building. You could just range them outside.

This was an all new deal for me. I had to make up big turkey feeders. They would be built on two big timbers for sled runners so you could pull them around. They were all made out of lumber. They would be ten feet long. They had to be two feet wide at the bottom and forty inches wide at the top. They had a V shaped bottom in them so the feed would run down and the turkeys could eat. These feeders would hold about two ton of feed. I made up enough to hold a big auger truckload. They would bring a load of pellets out and auger it in the wooden feeders.

Then there were the water troughs to make up. I took three 2 X 8s and nailed them together to make the troughs. I bought floats that would cut the water off when the trough got full. It took several thousand feet of three-fourth inch hose to run the hoses out to the turkey water troughs. I had to clean and disinfect every day. This took a lot of time.

Then I would walk through the turkeys and make sure there weren't any dead ones. It was a real important job to get the dead ones out of the pen. If you didn't the turkeys would eat on them and that would cause disease in the good turkeys.

The varmints would kill about one turkey every night. The turkeys didn't fly up in trees to roost. They were too heavy. They were on full feed and didn't know how to fly, so they just sat down on the ground at night. That was why the coons, opossums, and coyotes could get them so easy. We always ranged the bronze turkeys. They got a lot bigger than the white turkeys.

Back then we had several of the gobblers that got to weigh about fifty pounds at selling time. Selling time was always a big job to get enough help to load them out. We loaded them by hand. When we first started raising turkeys the turkey hauling trucks were loaded with wire cages about six feet high with small doors on every cage. We fixed up a ramp and drove the turkeys up the ramp.

Some of the workers were up next to the truck picking them up one at a time and putting them in the cages. One cage would hold about eight to ten turkeys. It always took five or six big semi trucks to haul them out. We usually ran several thousand at a time. We could raise two or three bunches a year. This was a lot of turkeys. The kids were sure good to help take care of them. This went on for about three or four years.

The turkey business was getting bigger and more modern, so most of the feed companies wanted you to build big turkey houses to raise the turkeys in. These buildings would have to be thirty to fifty feet wide and two hundred to five hundred feet long depending on how many turkeys you were going to raise. Then you would need that much or more building space to grow them on out. The turkey business was really changing. They were raising white turkeys instead of the old bronze turkeys.

# 1962

I decided it was time for me to get out of the turkey raising business. I am sure my whole family was glad when we quit raising turkeys. Life was back to normal again. We were just farming, raising cattle, horses, and a few hogs now and then.

This was about the time that the big white York hogs were getting started. In this part of the country they were sure big nice hogs. I got a chance to buy a few registered Yorks out of the north part of the state. They were sure good hogs. My, they had big litters and saved most of them. So hogs were good for a few years.

About ever so many years the market would go way down with hogs, cows, horses, grain, and everything else that the farmer raised. The farmer was the only people that had a product, took it to town, and someone else told him what he could get for his product. The farmer had always had to take whatever someone would give for his hogs, cattle, grain, or anything else he had to sell.

If a farmer goes to town and buys, he has to pay the price on the tag. Each item is marked a certain price. You have got to pay that price or you don't get the product. That is true with everything that the world has to sell. If I need a part for a tractor or machinery, it is always marked a certain price. I have to pay that price or I don't get the machinery parts. This never seemed right to me. The farmer raises much of the food for American people. So why does the government or big business get the right to tell the farmer what his product is worth? One day it might be a fair price and the next day it could be worth only half as much as it should be.

Today if I take hogs to market, they will bring maybe twenty-three or twenty four cents a pound. If I go to the store to buy a piece of pork, the cheapest thing will be over a dollar a pound and most of it is two to three dollars a pound. Something is really wrong. The farmer kept the old sow all year and fed her. Then she had pigs and he had to feed the little pigs for six to eight months before taking them to market. Maybe he would get twenty-five cents a pound. The government had put such strict regulations on everything that it cost so much more money.

The other side of the story was the union. It had gotten too big and strong. It started out to be a good thing but it got too big and out of control. The union was only a part of the work force of this country. A big part of the work force was the farmer and all of the land it took to raise those crops. The union didn't do anything to help the farmer out. In fact it was putting the farmer out of business. The farmers are the backbone of the United States but they have always had to take whatever the market would give them for their product.

The farmers had to keep the female of their livestock all year around so that they could raise more the next year. We had to work with our product all year. People in business kept their product a few days and maybe a few weeks and they would get paid union scale for their product. If the farmer had made union wages also the price of everything people had to buy would have doubled. Today a loaf of bread is $1.50 but it would be $3.00 a loaf. It would be the same with cereal and the price of meat, wool for clothing, and leather for shoes.

Not only has the government and union been a problem for the farmers, now the conservation is creating many new problems for the farmers. For years they have tried to get a bill passed that you have to fence off your small branches so cattle can't get in the water and drink. If you have a bigger creek that runs through your farm, they have tried to get a bill passed that anyone can come up and down your farm next to the creek to hunt or fish. When I go to the city, if I park for a couple of minutes on someone's property, they would give me a ticket.

> I can remember way back in the 1930s everybody burnt off their whole farm. In fact almost the whole county burnt every year. My, what good grass we had back then. The fires kept all the underbrush down and it didn't hurt the big trees.

I can remember way back in the 1930s everybody burnt off their whole farm. In fact almost the whole county burnt every year. My, what good grass we had back then. The fires kept all the underbrush down and it didn't hurt the big trees.

If you burnt every year there were not many leaves so the fire didn't get hot enough to kill the big timber. Now conservation has used their power to stop burning. They say we can't burn anymore.

Now there is 55 years of leaves and underbrush. The deer can't even get through. If you burnt off your land now it would kill all the big trees. We have seen this happen out west many times. Yellowstone National Park burned so badly there was hardly anything left. Since it began growing back everything looks healthier and better.

If the conservation would let the land be burnt off every year we would not see fires that kill all of our big timber. We would have big trees and open timber with lots of blue stem blue grass. We would have more wildlife roaming on the ranges in Benton County. Now instead of some good wildlife we have wild hogs. There are getting to be several of them. They have a real sharp and pointed nose. They can wedge their way through the underbrush pretty good. They can be very destructive and dangerous.

Someday God may take back our country and let nature do its job. It worked well when God created the universe.

# Biographical Sketch:

Glen Morton Harpham was born in Houstonia Missouri on September 17, 1925. As a young boy he grew up in the log cabin built by his grandfather, Charles Wesley Harpham. His childhood was spent helping out on the farm, raising livestock and growing crops, which would provide the family with food.

Glen attended school at the Antioch School house. He walked to school when he went. Often he was needed at home to help with the farm work.

In 1943, he was drafted into the army. He spent four years training and working in chemical warfare. He trained at Camp Sibert, Alabama for three months. Then he was shipped out to Guadalcanal where he guarded the U.S. chemical ammo site for three years. He was left on the island after the war to clean up the whole island. He had to survive much like the native people looking for food and water.

He spent most of his life working as a carpenter and farming. The family spent a few years raising turkeys, hogs, cattle, and there were always horses to ride. He and his wife Claudine raised their four children on a farm in Benton County not far from the homestead farm.

Glen and Claudine have served the Lord over fifty years. He serves as a deacon in the First Baptist Church of Climax Springs. His love for the Lord shows in his love for family, friends, and neighbors.

At age 80 Glen still lives on the Harpham homestead farm where he raises a few horses and cows. He began writing his story a few years ago so that his children and grandchildren could share in the rich heritage of their family.

www.ingramcontent.com/pod-product-compliance
Lightning Source LLC
Chambersburg PA
CBHW031121080526
44587CB00011B/1064